S. Hrg. 113–137

INTERNATIONAL DEVELOPMENT PRIORITIES IN THE FISCAL YEAR 2014 BUDGET

HEARING

BEFORE THE

COMMITTEE ON FOREIGN RELATIONS
UNITED STATES SENATE

ONE HUNDRED THIRTEENTH CONGRESS

FIRST SESSION

APRIL 24, 2013

Printed for the use of the Committee on Foreign Relations

Available via the World Wide Web: http://www.gpo.gov/fdsys/

U.S. GOVERNMENT PRINTING OFFICE

86–148 PDF   WASHINGTON : 2014

COMMITTEE ON FOREIGN RELATIONS

ROBERT MENENDEZ, New Jersey, *Chairman*

BARBARA BOXER, California
BENJAMIN L. CARDIN, Maryland
ROBERT P. CASEY, JR., Pennsylvania
JEANNE SHAHEEN, New Hampshire
CHRISTOPHER A. COONS, Delaware
RICHARD J. DURBIN, Illinois
TOM UDALL, New Mexico
CHRISTOPHER MURPHY, Connecticut
TIM KAINE, Virginia

BOB CORKER, Tennessee
JAMES E. RISCH, Idaho
MARCO RUBIO, Florida
RON JOHNSON, Wisconsin
JEFF FLAKE, Arizona
JOHN McCAIN, Arizona
JOHN BARRASSO, Wyoming
RAND PAUL, Kentucky

DANIEL E. O'BRIEN, *Staff Director*
LESTER E. MUNSON III, *Republican Staff Director*

(II)

CONTENTS

(III)

INTERNATIONAL DEVELOPMENT PRIORITIES IN THE FISCAL YEAR 2014 BUDGET

WEDNESDAY, APRIL 24, 2013

U.S. SENATE,
COMMITTEE ON FOREIGN RELATIONS,
Washington, DC.

The committee met, pursuant to notice, at 10:01 a.m., in room SD–419, Dirksen Senate Office Building, Hon. Robert Menendez (chairman of the committee) presiding.

Present: Senators Menendez, Cardin, Casey, Coons, Udall, Murphy, Kaine, Corker, and Rubio.

OPENING STATEMENT OF HON. ROBERT MENENDEZ, U.S. SENATOR FROM NEW JERSEY

The CHAIRMAN. Good morning. This hearing of the Senate Foreign Relations Committee will come to order.

Today we welcome Administrator Shah of the USAID before the committee. We look forward to your perspective on making certain that U.S. development assistance is carefully calibrated with our overall U.S. foreign policy priorities.

We all know the rapidly evolving landscape in the Middle East and Africa and the Asia-Pacific region demands that we continue to invest in programs and relationships that advance our strategic interests and basic values. Even in this age of fiscal austerity with the significant budgetary limitations we face, it is my view that the benefits of such investments far outweigh the costs, and it is the men and women at USAID who see the results of those investments firsthand every day.

In 2011, you described "having seen famine for the first time in the world's largest refugee camp 50 miles from the Somali border after the worst drought in 60 years," as you described, "had thrown 13.3 million people into crisis and bought more than 750,000 people, mostly women and children, to the brink of starvation."

You mentioned meeting mothers who had carried their children for weeks across famine-stricken and terrorist-held lands, and a young Somali mother named Habida who walked 100 kilometers to the nearest camp and had to decide which of her two children she would leave behind because she could not carry both, a heartbreaking image that leaves no one unmoved by the suffering. And we commend you and all the men and women at AID for working very hard every day around the world to end it.

Today I hope to hear from you about how we can do even more with the limited funds we have to maximize the effectiveness of development aid and what more we can do to reform programs that enhance relationships that will advance U.S. interests and values around the world.

Your creativity and energy has been essential to the reform process, but it is also important, however, that Congress remain a working partner with you to establish our international development priorities and ensure that all reforms focus on best practices and results as well, that they be well crafted, and will have the hoped-for effects.

I am looking forward to an ongoing conversation with you about how to get the best results for USAID for our foreign assistance, for donors, for NGOs, and for the taxpayers.

USAID Forward is an example of a reform that has achieved results. It aligns resources with priorities, builds capacity through sustainable development, and identifies new innovations to help meet the President's goal of ending poverty in the next two decades. I applaud the progress USAID Forward is making, but more needs to be done to institutionalize reforms in cooperation with the Congress to make certain they reflect our overall foreign policy, our international development priorities, and pay dividends around the world in every region.

And so I look forward to your testimony. I will have the rest of my statement entered into the record.

Having said all of those great, positive things, I do not want you to believe that there are not some issues that I have some concerns about, as I expressed to you. But certainly the work at AID has been exceptional, and we applaud your for it.

[The prepared statement of Chairman Robert Menendez follows:]

PREPARED STATEMENT OF SENATOR ROBERT MENENDEZ

INTRODUCTION—PRAISE FOR THE WORK OF USAID

Thank you, Administrator Shah, for coming before the committee. We look forward to your perspective on making certain that U.S. development assistance is carefully calibrated with our overall U.S. foreign policy priorities.

We all know that the rapidly evolving landscape in the Middle East, Africa, and the Asia-Pacific demands that we continue to invest in programs and relationships that advance our strategic interests and basic values.

Even in this age of fiscal austerity—with the significant budgetary limitations we face—it is my view, that the benefits of such investments far outweigh the costs . . . and it is the men and women at USAID who see the results of those investments firsthand, every day.

In 2011, you described ''having seen famine for the first time at the world's largest refugee camp—50 miles from the Somali border—after the worst drought in 60 years had . . .''—as you described—''. . . thrown 13.3 million people into crisis and brought more than 750,000 people—mostly women and children—to the brink of starvation.''

You mentioned meeting ''mothers who had carried their children for weeks across famine-stricken and terrorist-held lands . . .'' and a young Somali mother named Habiba who walked 100 kilometers to the nearest camp and had to decide which of her two children she would leave behind because she could not carry both.

A heartbreaking image that leaves no one unmoved by the suffering—and we commend you and all of the men and women at USAID for working hard every day—round the world—to end it.

Today, I hope to hear from you how we can do even more—with the limited funds we have—to maximize the effectiveness of development aid and what more we can do to reform programs and enhance relationships that will advance U.S. interests and values around the world.

USAID REFORMS

Your creativity and energy has been essential to the reform process . . . but it is also important that Congress remain a working partner with you to establish our international development priorities and assure that all reforms focus on best practices and results, are well-crafted, and will have the hoped-for effects.

I look forward to an ongoing conversation with you about how to get the best results for USAID, for our foreign assistance, for donors, for NGOs, and for the taxpayer.

USAID Forward is an example of a reform that has gotten results—it aligns resources with priorities, builds capacity through sustainable development, and identifies new innovations to help meet the President's goal of ending poverty in the next two decades.

I applaud the progress USAID Forward is making, but more needs to be done to institutionalize reforms—in cooperation with Congress—to make certain they reflect our overall foreign policy, our international development priorities, and pay dividends around the world—in every region.

CONCLUSION—WE CAN DO MORE

In my view, even within the confines of our budgetary limitations, we can do more in Syria—though we're already the world's largest donor nation—to increase the level of humanitarian support because—clearly—we have to do more to address the world's most pressing humanitarian crisis—with 4 million displaced and 700,000 dead.

We can do more in the Sahel to mitigate the suffering . . . more to alleviate horrific conditions in the long-suffering communities of Somali refugees, displaced Congolese . . . more to combat AIDS, tuberculosis, polio, and malaria . . . more to provide simple tools that can prevent millions of childhood deaths . . . critical to our global health strategy . . . more to help others take the reigns of leadership in their own countries . . . And—I believe—we can reach 2 to 4 million more hungry people if we maximize efficiency in how we provide food aid.

It seems to me that a common sense, achievable approach to Food Aid Reform is to work with U.S. farmers, labor, and experts in the field to improve not only how we deliver resources in times of crisis, but how we promote food security and resilience in mitigating emergencies.

Again, let me commend the men and women at USAID for their service to the Nation and for meeting our international development priorities by doing so much for so many around the world.

Thank you, Administrator Shah.

The CHAIRMAN. Let me turn to the ranking member, Senator Corker, for his comments.

OPENING STATEMENT OF HON. BOB CORKER, U.S. SENATOR FROM TENNESSEE

Senator CORKER. Thank you, Mr. Chairman, and thanks for having the hearing. Mr. Shah, thank you for being here and for your openness in dealing with our office and others.

In this fiscal environment, obviously looking at how we deliver aid is very important, and I know you have done so.

And I appreciate the time, again, that your staff has spent with ours.

I do applaud you, as the chairman just did, on your movements in the food assistance areas. It looks like, if I read correctly, about 55 percent of our programs are being transferred over to this new approach. I would love to see you go to 100 when it is appropriate. I know you have political considerations back home relative to that, but I do applaud those efforts.

And I will say that at the same for decades, we have been providing food assistance, and we still are in the mode of, you know, day-to-day assistance. And so I do hope either today or over time you will cause us to explain why after so many decades of doing what we are doing we are still in the situation in so many countries where, you know, we are still having to provide day-to-day assistance, and they do not have the capacity themselves to do what needs to be done there.

But again, I think you have taken a very positive step.

I thank you for that and looking forward to working with you toward that end.

Another area we have talked with you and your staff about is just development, which takes place in areas which are not secure. I know we had a huge amount of problems in Iraq. We are going to have probably even greater problems once people get through looking at what we did in Afghanistan. And I know that it is very difficult for civilians to be out with development projects in areas that are not secure. We understand that.

My sense is that we are going to be very soon at some point dealing with the same kind of issues in Syria, and I do hope that we will continue discussions about the best way to make sure that those kinds of development programs are monitored properly when it is so difficult for your outstanding staff to be able to get in and deal with that. So a big issue.

I also welcome the fact that your agency talked about most Caribbean and Latin American countries graduating from aid by the year 2030. I do hope that that is not just a rhetorical statement, but there is a plan to make that happen. And again, I thank you for having that type of goal, but we would like to see the backup and the vision that is going to cause that to occur.

And then I will close with this, which is the same thing we talked to Secretary Kerry about. Look, a lot of money is going out of USAID. I know compared to our overall budget, it is not as much as people in our country think. But we need a permanent inspector general, OK? I do expect you very soon to send up a highly qualified, capable inspector general. Acting inspectors general do not have the clout that permanent inspectors general do, and it is just not responsible. So I hope very soon that the status on this will change.

Again, thank you for being here, and thank you for your service to our country.

The CHAIRMAN. With that, Administrator, we welcome your remarks.

STATEMENT OF HON. RAJIV SHAH, ADMINISTRATOR, U.S. AGENCY FOR INTERNATIONAL DEVELOPMENT, WASHINGTON, DC

Dr. SHAH. Thank you, Chairman Menendez, and thank you, Ranking Member Corker. I am personally very appreciative for the opportunity to be here to discuss the President's fiscal year 2014 budget. And I am very grateful for the counsel, guidance, and oversight that you have offered and continue to offer on a personal basis, and from your team and your staff. So I appreciate this unique opportunity.

I would ask that my formal remarks are entered for the record, and will just briefly summarize a few topline points.

This is an important moment for development, and I was eager to hear in both of your statements that basic reflection as we draw down from a decade of war. We are rethinking how we project power and American values around the world in a manner that keeps us safe and improves our own domestic and economic opportunities.

President Obama and Secretary Kerry, like Secretary Clinton before him, have talked about elevating development as part of our national security and foreign policy strategy, including with a real focus on America's economic competitiveness over time.

I was grateful, Senator Menendez, for your mention of the reference and the visit to the Somalia refugee camp. That was an eye-opening experience and one that I will never forget. I was a few months ago back in Somalia, and this time instead of seeing the devastating human consequences of a famine with children literally dying in front of our eyes, we saw a much more hopeful picture. We saw American investments in a new government and a new flourishing civil society start to yield some results as street lights came on in Mogadishu for the first time in several decades and citizens celebrated peacefully for the first time that most could remember.

We noted that we were helping more than 400 local communities improve their agriculture and helping people leave the displacement camps that were formed around Mogadishu during the famine, to go back to their communities, start growing their own food, and start rebuilding their own lives, because the purpose of our partnership should not be to perpetuate dependence, but to build self-sufficiency and human dignity.

We are helping in more than 40 small-scale fishing ports to replace piracy with transparent and legal small-scale fishing activity. And those are the types of partnerships that will help establish stability, security, and peace in that critical region.

Those examples are emblematic of what we believe is an approach that focuses on ensuring that development builds self-sufficiency and dignity and replaces dependency. It is an approach that we believe is delivering real results. Our Feed the Future Program and partnership involved us making tough decisions. We cut agricultural programs in 23 countries in order to focus in 19 that were willing to make reforms and expand their own investment.

We are now beginning to see the results. In those 19 countries, poverty has been reduced by 5.6 percent on an annual basis. Seven million farm households directly benefit from American investments in their agriculture, science, and technology. More than $3½ billion have been committed to invest in a subset of these countries so that private and commercial interests can help transform and end hunger in those settings. And all of this has been coupled with real policy reforms that require our country partners to invest more resources to fight corruption and to establish policies that are friendly to business investment.

We are seeing similar results in our efforts to end preventable child death. Again, we made tough decisions to cut 22 country programs in global health in order to focus in those countries that have the greatest burden of disease. This effort is seeing a real reduction in the rate of child death as it is reduced from 7.6 million kids under the age of 5 to 6.9 million today. We believe we can end preventable child deaths within two decades, and are committed to that model.

We are also seeing that effort take hold in our citizen security efforts in our own hemisphere. In El Salvador, we recently launched the largest public-private partnership in the region where we made a $20 million investment, but that unlocked more than $22 million of investment from local foundations and local businesses because it is those local institutions that believe that addressing citizen security is the key to unlocking greater business investment and growth in that critical part of the world.

These new efforts have been possible because of your support; your support for USAID Forward and a new model of partnering with local partners, a new model of innovating with scientists and technologists who can help bring the costs down and help us aspire to achieve bigger outcomes, and your partnership in measuring and reporting on results.

I am pleased to note that today the United States has joined the International Aid Transparency Initiative and our aid data is increasingly transparent and accessible to everyone. You can go to the App store and download an application that has much of our evaluation data, easily accessible and unadulterated, so we can all learn together from an evidence base that defines what works and what does not as we make these critical investments abroad.

As part of this transition, this year's budget includes an important proposal to reform the way we provide food assistance around the world. The President's proposal is designed to help us reach 4 million additional hungry children with basic nutrition interventions, and to target those feeding programs to those kids when they need it most and when it can have the most impact on improving their ability to grow and thrive.

The approach will expand the flexibility we need to meet needs in a changing world, a world where increasingly humanitarian catastrophes happen alongside security challenges, whether it is in opposition controlled parts of Syria or al-Shabaab controlled parts of Somalia. And it is an approach that maintains and, in fact, renews a partnership, an important partnership, with American agriculture that will allow us to refocus on creating new high nutrition and modern agricultural products and foods that can be targeted to kids in a way that saves their lives. We thank you for your reflections on this proposal and your consideration.

Finally, I would like to thank our staff. Around the world we now have 9,600 staff, many of which carry different types of acronyms or hiring authorities, but all of whom bring passion and a commitment to this incredible mission; a mission of representing our country around the world and working to end extreme poverty and to protect those who are most vulnerable.

In this past year, cognizant of the risks that many of our staff do take, as Senator Corker highlighted, we lost one of our own, Ragaei Abdelfattah, in Afghanistan. And one of our toughest moments as an agency was getting through that very trying period, and we reflect on and thank Ragaei and his family for their service.

At a time when cuts across our Government are significant and having real impacts, the fiscal year 2014 request reflects a 6-percent decrease compared to the fiscal year 2012 enacted budget.

We are making very tough tradeoffs around the world in order to focus on delivering results and are cognizant of the economic and budget times that we live in.

But we are also focused on doing things differently, on demanding more of others, and on partnering better to achieve better results. And it is our belief that with this new approach taking hold, we can still have big aspirations, and that is why the President highlighted our capacity to help end extreme poverty in two decades. It is why we believe by projecting American values effectively around the world we can support transitions in the Middle East, help bring our troops home from Afghanistan, help improve trade and economic ties in Latin America, and help expand on our engagements in Africa, including connecting American businesses to real growth opportunities there, while simultaneously working to do things like ending preventable child deaths.

I thank you and look forward to your questions, comments, and thoughts as we go forward. Thank you.

[The prepared statement of Dr. Shah follows:]

PREPARED STATEMENT OF DR. RAJIV SHAH

Thank you, Chairman Menendez, Ranking Member Corker, and members of the committee. I am pleased to join you to discuss the President's fiscal year 2014 budget request for USAID.

In his State of the Union Address, President Obama called upon our Nation to join with the world in ending extreme poverty in the next two decades. Today, we have new tools that enable us to achieve a goal that was simply unimaginable in the past: the eradication of extreme poverty and its most devastating corollaries, including widespread hunger and preventable child and maternal deaths.

The President's fiscal year 2014 budget request responds to this call and the most critical development challenges of our time. It supports important global partnerships, including the New Alliance for Food Security and Nutrition and the Child Survival Call to Action, by increasing and focusing investments in food security and maternal and child health. It builds resilience in areas besieged by recurrent crisis and natural disaster, with a focus on the Horn of Africa and Sahel regions. And it advances a comprehensive food aid reform package that will enable us to feed 2 to 4 million additional people each year.

The President's request enables USAID to strategically advance our national security priorities by implementing critical economic growth, democracy, human rights, and governance programs in the Middle East and North Africa, as well as in support of the administration's Asia-Pacific Rebalance. It also focuses activities in Afghanistan, Pakistan, and Iraq at an appropriate level to sustain the gains we have made in those countries over the last decade. And it strengthens economic prosperity, both at home and abroad.

The President's request also makes important investments in Latin America by expanding economic opportunity and social equity and strengthening citizen security by promoting effective judicial systems and investing in communities and at-risk youth to address the root causes of crime. Some of USAID's most exciting examples of fostering innovation are in this region, where, through groundbreaking public-private partnerships, we have broadened local investment for development.

I want to highlight how the investments we make in foreign assistance, which represents just 1 percent of the Federal budget, help our country respond to the global challenges we face and how we have modernized our Agency to deliver results that shape a safer and more prosperous future.

A NEW MODEL FOR DEVELOPMENT: PARTNERSHIPS, INNOVATION, AND RESULTS

The FY 2014 request for USAID managed, or partially managed, accounts is $20.4 billion, 6 percent below the total enacted funding for FY 2012. In this tough budget environment, USAID is committed to maximizing the value of every dollar. We have made tough choices so that we are working where we will have greatest impact, and shifting personnel and funding resources toward programs that will achieve the most meaningful results. Since 2010, regional program areas have been reduced by

29 percent, Feed the Future agriculture programs have been phased out of 22 countries, and USAID global health program areas have been phased out of 23 countries. The President's FY 2014 request continues to build on gains we have made over the past year to work smarter and more effectively through a suite of ambitious reforms called USAID Forward. Through USAID Forward, the Agency has fostered new partnerships, placing a greater emphasis on innovation, and a relentless focus on results. These reforms have formed the foundation of a new model for development that continues to define the way we work around the world.

The FY 2014 budget provides funding to mobilize a new generation of innovators and scientists. Through our Development Innovations Ventures, we invite problem-solvers everywhere to contribute a cost-effective and cutting-edge idea that could scale to reach millions.

It provides funding for Grand Challenges for Development, capitalizing on the success of previous challenges to accelerate reductions in maternal and child mortality, promote childhood literacy, power agriculture through clean energy, and raise the voices of all citizens through technology. We have received more than 500 applications per challenge, with almost 50 percent of innovations coming from developing and emerging economies. For example, through ''All Children Reading: A Grand Challenge for Development,'' nearly three dozen organizations—half of them local—are pioneering a range of novel approaches to education, from helping children in India learn to read with same language subtitling on movies and TV to bringing fully stocked e-readers to rural Ghana.

The request accelerates advances of USAID's Higher Education Solutions Network, a constellation of seven development innovation labs on university campuses that work with a global network of partners to provide solutions for key development challenges, leveraging tens of millions of dollars of university and private-sector financing.

The 2014 request also allows us to work more effectively with a range of partners, from faith-based organizations to private sector companies. A new focus on leveraging private sector resources has enabled us to dramatically expand our Development Credit Authority—unlocking a record $524 million in FY 2012 in commercial capital to empower entrepreneurs around the world. Last year alone, we increased our contributions to public-private partnerships by almost 40 percent, leveraging an additional $383 million.

This funding also allows us to rigorously measure and evaluate our work so we know which of our development efforts are effective and which we need to scale back or modify. Since the launch of our evaluation policy, 186 high-quality evaluations have been completed and are available on our Web site or through a mobile ''app'' that is easily downloaded. Half of these evaluations have led to mid-course corrections and one-third has led to budget changes.

A new emphasis on supporting local solutions has enabled us to shift $745 million in funding to local institutions, firms, and organizations in the last year alone—helping replace aid with self-sufficiency. When we partner with developing country institutions, we use sophisticated tools to assess their financial management capacity and safeguard U.S. resources.

As part of our new model, we're insisting our partners make policy reforms and fight corruption in order to meet the conditions of our assistance. Through new models of partnership that demand mutual accountability—including the New Alliance for Food Security and Nutrition and the Tokyo Mutual Accountability Framework for Afghanistan—we are creating incentives for governments to strengthen their own institutions.

Across our work, we are moving from a traditional approach of top-down development to a new model that engages talent and innovation everywhere to achieve extraordinary goals. In education, a core development objective, we are harnessing this new approach to help close the gaps in access and quality of education. We know that globally 171 million people could be lifted out of poverty if all students in low-income countries gained basic literacy. Our strategy for basic education is focused on improving reading skills for 100 million children in primary grades by 2015 and increasing equitable access to education in crisis and conflict environments for 15 million learners by 2015.

FOOD AID REFORM

At its foundation, our new model of development shares the bedrock principles of effectiveness and efficiency that serve as the clarion call for government today.

There is perhaps no better example of this fundamental imperative than the food aid reform package proposed in this year's budget request, which would enable us to feed 2 to 4 million more hungry men, women and children every year with the same resources, while maintaining the valuable contribution of American agriculture to this mission.

Through P.L. 480 Title II, or Food for Peace, America's agricultural bounty and generosity have fed well over a billion people in more than 150 countries since 1954. But while the world has changed significantly since Title II was created, our hallmark food assistance program has not. The current program limits our ability to use the appropriate tools for each humanitarian situation—tools we know will help people faster and at a lesser cost.

Buying food locally can speed the arrival of aid by as many as 14 weeks—making up precious time when every day can mean the difference between life and death. It can also cost much less—as much as 50 percent less for cereals alone. In complex environments such as Syria and Somalia, which are increasingly the kind of crises where we need to provide assistance, these more flexible tools are invaluable.

The more agile, flexible, and modern approach laid out in the President's budget request pairs the continued purchase of the best of American agriculture with greater flexibility around interventions such as local procurement, cash transfers, and electronic vouchers. The President's proposal maintains the majority of our emergency food aid funds—55 percent in 2014—for the purchase and transport of American commodities. That means we're going to keep working with soy, wheat, pulse, and rice farmers and processors across America who help feed hungry children from Bangladesh to the Sahel—often in the form of specialized high nutrition products.

At a time of urgent human need and budget constraints, we can save more lives without asking for more money.

The proposal also reaffirms our commitment to development partners who receive Title II funding, enabling them to provide the same types of development programs at a lower cost. These programs strengthen our ability to reduce chronic poverty, build resilience, and help prevent future crises.

FEED THE FUTURE

Ending hunger and creating a food secure world are vital components of the fight to end extreme poverty. Launched in 2009 by President Obama, Feed the Future is unlocking agricultural growth, helping transform developing economies and ending the cycle of food crises and emergency food aid. Although the initiative is still in its early days, we are beginning to see significant results.

In Rwanda, we have reached 1.6 million children under 5 with nutrition programs that reduced anemia, supported community gardens, and treated acute malnutrition. In Bangladesh, we helped more than 400,000 rice farmers increase yields by 15 percent through the more efficient use of fertilizer, which led to the first-ever rice surplus in the country's poorest state. In FY 2012, we helped more than 7 million farmers across the world apply these kinds of new technologies and practices, four times the number we reached the previous year.

The FY 2014 request provides $269 million for the President's G8 commitment to the New Alliance for Food Security and Nutrition, which aims to lift 50 million people in sub-Saharan Africa out of poverty in the next decade. Since its inception at last year's G8 summit, we have helped leverage more than $3.75 billion in commitments from more than 70 global and local companies. In Tanzania, Yara International is constructing a fertilizer terminal at the nation's largest port, and, in Ethiopia, DuPont is expanding seed distribution to reach 35,000 smallholder maize farmers and increase productivity by 50 percent.

At the same time, participating African governments have committed to serious market-oriented reforms. Tanzania has removed its export ban on staple commodities, Mozambique eliminated permit requirements for interdistrict trade, and Ethiopia no longer imposes export quotas on commercial farm outputs and processed goods.

GLOBAL HEALTH

Thanks to strong bipartisan support we are on track to provide life-saving health assistance to more people than ever before. The FY 2014 Global Health request supports our goals of creating an AIDS-free generation, ending preventable child and maternal death, and protecting communities from infectious diseases.

Across our global health portfolio, we are aligning our budgets to the areas of greatest need. Now, 90 percent of USAID bilateral maternal and child health funding is in the 24 USAID priority countries that account for three-quarters of maternal and child deaths.

The request supports the continuation and scale-up of high-impact HIV/AIDS prevention, care, and treatment tools in pursuit of an AIDS-free generation. The request also provides $1.65 billion under PEPFAR for the U.S. contribution to the Global Fund to Fight AIDS, Tuberculosis, and Malaria.

In June, USAID cohosted a Call to Action to accelerate progress and end preventable child death. A powerful example of how our new model of development can rally diverse partners behind ambitious but achievable goals, the Call to Action has encouraged more than 170 countries, 200 civil society organizations, and 220 faith-based organizations to sign a pledge to help reduce child mortality. This global effort builds on an 8-percent reduction we have seen from 2008 to 2011 in child mortality in countries where the U.S. Government provides assistance.

We will continue to fund critical efforts in voluntary family planning, immunizations, nutrition, malaria, tuberculosis, and neglected tropical diseases—cost-effective interventions that save lives, while preventing the spread of disease.

SUPPORTING STRATEGIC PRIORITIES AND STRENGTHENING NATIONAL SECURITY

Across the world, we are strengthening democracy, human rights, and governance, with a special emphasis on marginalized populations, including women and youth. Support for democratic and economic transitions enables the rise of capable new players who can help solve regional challenges and advance U.S. national security.

Since January 2011, the State Department and USAID have allocated more than $1.8 billion to support democratic transitions in the Middle East and North Africa and respond to emerging crisis needs in the region. The President's Request of $580 million for the Middle East and North Africa Incentive Fund provides support to citizen demands for change, improves our ability to respond adroitly to new challenges and opportunities, and begins to address the imbalance between our security and economic assistance in the region.

The budget request supports our humanitarian assistance work around the globe in places where the need is greatest. This is particularly true in Syria, where at least 4 million people are in need of humanitarian assistance and 2 million are displaced. To date, State and USAID have provided nearly $385 million in humanitarian relief to the Syrian people.

In Iraq, Afghanistan and Pakistan, USAID continues to work closely with interagency partners including the State and Defense Departments, to move toward long-term stability, promote economic growth, and support democratic reforms, including the rights of women. Despite the challenges, we have seen a number of positive gains. For example, over the past decade in Afghanistan, we have increased access to education, resulting in dramatic increases in primary school enrollment from 900,000 boys in 2002 to 8 million students in 2012, 37 percent of whom are girls. In Iraq, USAID-funded legal clinics have supported over 1,700 legal cases on behalf of vulnerable individuals, including internally displaced persons and ethnic and religious minorities.

The President's budget request supports the administration's Asia-Pacific Rebalance by increasing funding for the region to address critical gaps in core programs to renew U.S. leadership, deepen economic ties, promote democratic and universal values, and strengthen diplomatic engagement. In addition, we are seizing new opportunities for partnership in Asia, including in Burma, a nation undertaking political and economic reform.

GLOBAL CLIMATE CHANGE AND BUILDING RESILIENCE

As a result of global climate change, natural disasters are becoming more frequent and more severe. With a new emphasis on helping vulnerable communities build resilience to disasters, the Global Climate Change Presidential Initiative invests in developing countries to accelerate transitions to climate-resilient, low-emission economic growth, while incentivizing private sector investment to scale impact and sustain progress. For example, we are partnering with the Consumer Goods Forum—which represents about 400 companies and $3 trillion in market value—to reduce tropical deforestation from key commodities, like palm oil and timber.

Drawing on lessons learned during last year's food crisis in the Horn of Africa—as well as decades of experience responding to disasters—USAID is pioneering a fundamental new approach to help communities strengthen their resilience in the face of crises. In Ethiopia, for instance, we're working with international firms like Swiss Re and local businesses to develop index-based livestock insurance—a new product that uses satellite data to protect pastoralists from drought-related losses.

CONCLUSION

When people around the globe cannot feed their families, when young adults find themselves without education or a source of income, and when parents watch their children die of preventable illnesses, the world is inherently less secure. The FY 2014 budget request will continue our work to combat these causes of instability and end extreme poverty.

These investments aren't just from the American people; they're for the American people. By promoting sustainable growth in the developing world, we spur new markets abroad and energize our economy here at home. By driving innovations in agriculture, education, and global health, we strengthen global stability and advance our national security. And by delivering aid in the wake of natural disasters and humanitarian crises, we express the generosity and goodwill that unite us as a people.

The CHAIRMAN. Thank you, Administrator, and your full statement will be entered into the record.

Let me start off. You know, I took my first trip as chairman to Afghanistan and Pakistan because I believe it is still obviously a vital national security interest to the United States. And the region is in the midst of economic security and political transition. And during our trip there, I spent time with our aid missions and conducted a couple of field visits to visit some of our programs. And I am incredibly impressed with the dedication and drive of our teams there.

But I also have concerns as to how we conduct oversight in the field given the security conditions, so my questions are in this regard. Are we right sizing our aid presence in both countries to reflect our diminishing footprint or our security concerns and implementation challenges? And specifically, what steps are taken to ensure that our aid is necessary, achievable, and sustainable, which are steps that this committee called for in its June 2011 oversight report?

Dr. SHAH. Thank you, Senator, and I want to thank you personally for your leadership on this issue and for taking the time to meet with our staff when you were there. That meant a lot to them and was very encouraging for them to personally get the chance to meet with you.

As you note, the gains in Afghanistan that we believe have resulted from our collective international investments have been real and significant, and now create the opportunity for some degree of stability as our troops start to come home. We have seen 9 percent annualized growth rates year on year for the past decade. The largest increases in human longevity and reductions in child and maternal mortality anywhere in the world have been experienced in Afghanistan in part due to our investments in health.

We have 8 million kids in school, nearly 35 percent of whom are girls compared to no girls in school under the previous Taliban regime. And energy access has more than tripled as a result of collective investments we have made, and we have put down more than 1,900 kilometers of new road in partnership with the people and businesses and governments of Afghanistan.

But it has taken a lot to make sure that this program has become more accountable and more transparent in the last few years. When we took office, we launched an effort called the A–3 Initiative, Accountable Assistance for Afghanistan, which included a full partner vetting of all of our partners and subcontractors. It included getting eyes and third-party monitors on most major programs and investments. It included a local cost auditing system that allowed us to understand where resources were going and how performance was improving.

We believe that some of those efforts will be at risk as we see a transition that will limit, to some degree, our capacity to be physically present and out in all parts of Afghanistan, seeing and engaging on these projects and programs. I spoke to General Dunford earlier this week by videoconference, and it is part of our coordinated civilian military plan to make sure that we have a capacity to continue to oversee these programs effectively. But we know we will be doing it with some degree of reduced staffing, with more local staff, with more support from the Afghan Public Protection Force, and with other forms of ensuring accountability for our resources.

So I thank you for asking that question. It is something that we are working on aggressively right now.

The CHAIRMAN. So do you believe that the programs moving forward in that region will continue to be able to follow those three criteria that the committee set, particularly sustainability?

Dr. SHAH. Absolutely, and, in fact, those criteria become more important, not less important, going forward. If programs cannot sustain themselves anymore, they are really not worth doing because we know that we are not going to be there endlessly.

We did, in fact, pull together the international community in Tokyo last year, and we got the international community to commit $16 billion of development investment for Afghanistan over the next 4 to 5 years. As part of that, we introduced a mutual accountability framework with the Government of Afghanistan, and so they have to show real progress on corruption, on asset recoveries from Kabul Bank, on pursuing with clarity and transparency fair and free elections in order for those resources to take hold and for those pledges to be met.

We are doing that not unilaterally, but in concert with 20 other international partners. And we believe that sort of approach—real mutual accountability on behalf of ourselves and our Afghan partners—will be critical if we are going to effectively over time replace aid and assistance with business and investment.

The CHAIRMAN. Which brings me to the question of capability— USAID went through, in my view, a 20-year decline in personnel and dispersion of development responsibilities to other entities, such as the Millennium Challenge Corporation, the State Department AID's coordinator, and in 2006, the loss of budgeting and policy capabilities. How would you assess your agency's progress in restoring its capacities under USAID Forward and the development and leadership initiative? And, you know, describe for me your goals—the end goals of these efforts as you move forward, because one of the things I want to understand I have been an advocate of is making sure that USAID has the wherewithal, and the ability, and the personnel to carry out its mission. And I think the dispersal that we have seen, particularly including Defense Department engagement in what, in essence, was development activities, undermine the capacity.

Dr. SHAH. Thank you, Senator, and thank you for your personal advocacy on behalf of those objectives.

Our end goal very clearly is to be the world's premiere development enterprise, and I believe we are well on the way to accomplishing that. Our focus on public-private partnerships has been unique and extraordinarily effective in many parts of the world.

We have been able to rebuild our budget authority, our policy capacity. We have hired 1,100 new staff because of the Development Leadership Initiative on which you commented. And we believe these investments, deployed accurately, particularly on contract oversight and accountability, are saving taxpayer dollars on the program side of our budget.

So we believe these are important investments that need to continue to be made. They are put at real risk and threatened by current sequestration realities. The fiscal year 2014 budget includes an investment in our operating expenses that will allow us to continue on this path of rebuilding this agency. But we have had real success in the last 3 years with strong support from President Obama and Secretary Clinton, and now Secretary Kerry.

The CHAIRMAN. All right. I will come back to some of my concerns in the next round.

Senator.

Senator CORKER. Thank you, Mr. Chairman. Again, Mr. Shah, thank you for being here and for your work in bringing some of the private sector, Gates Foundation, thinking to USAID. It is much appreciated.

Will you go ahead and tell me what you plan to do on the inspector general? I would imagine in the next 2 weeks you plan to send up a permanent nominee.

Dr. SHAH. Well, we have had a very good working relationship with our acting inspector general, and the White House, of course, has responsibility for putting forward a Presidential nomination. We know that that process is, and has been, well under way, and do expect very soon for the White House to make that nomination.

Senator CORKER. I noticed you and the administration have decided that 55 percent of our food aid is going to be spent here in the United States. How did you decide on that number?

Dr. SHAH. Well, first, thank you for your leadership and comments on food aid specifically.

As we look around the world, we note that over the last few years, the program has had essentially about 81 percent of the program tied to the purchase and distribution on U.S.-flag vessels of American commodities, which gives us a little bit of flexibility, about 19 percent, every year. That flexibility has been deployed in different places.

This year, with the challenges of providing humanitarian assistance in and around Syria, that flexibility is being absorbed almost completely in that setting and in that region. As a result, there are a number of other countries—the Democratic Republic of Congo, Somalia, and Pakistan—where we actually have to take children off of nutrition support, often in post-famine or post-hunger situations, because we are reverting from a more efficient locally procured program to the more traditional U.S.-based program. And there are 155,000 kids in Somalia that this year will be subject to that.

So we basically looked at how do we avoid that outcome, how can we build maximum flexibility and efficiency? And we want to also have a renewed partnership with American agriculture, a partnership that prioritizes high nutrition food products that America ought to have the scientific and technical lead in producing, a partnership that is flexible and efficient in how we get those products to people quickly in times of great need, and a partnership that continues to benefit from the engagement from the agricultural communities in this country that sustain this effort over time.

So that is how we ended up with the proposal we have. We believe the proposal will allow in the first year to reach 4 million additional children.

Senator CORKER. And so your goal, though, still over time is self-sufficiency. Is that correct?

Dr. SHAH. Absolutely. The goal—as the President has said over and over since 2009 when he first launched Feed the Future, our goal is to move people from food aid to self-sufficiency so they can be trading and commercial partners with us. As we have seen, our largest recipient of American food aid in the 1960s and 1970s was South Korea, and today they are obviously a major trading partner.

Senator CORKER. Do you plan on working with this committee to get the reforms you are putting in place into code, or are you just going to do the easy route of going and talking with an appropriator and getting it done in that manner?

Dr. SHAH. Absolutely, sir; we would be eager to work with this committee to have as much structure and longevity and commitment to this renewed vision of an efficient, effective, and more high-impact results-oriented program.

Senator CORKER. Really the only way to lock in the reforms is to get us to get it into code, right? And you know that it is going to be there when you go off to do other things, some other place?

Dr. SHAH. Yes, sir.

Senator CORKER. Let me talk to you a little bit about Syria. I wrote an op-ed this morning that was about our role in Syria. And obviously there are multiple things that need to be done there to change the balance of power. What do you think, briefly, USAID can do to change the balance right now to favor the more moderate secular opposition groups that are inside Syria?

Dr. SHAH. Well, thank you, Senator, for your leadership on Syria and articulating that as the central challenge. I think Secretary Kerry also has acknowledged that that is our goal.

And I would point out that with 4½ million internally displaced and 1½ million refugees already, that we have a major humanitarian and political crisis on our hands.

In terms of your specific question of how can we tip the balance toward what we think of more moderate and more responsible within the framework of the opposition, Secretary Kerry announced this past weekend a doubling of our aid and assistance to the Syrian Opposition Council. As part of that commitment to them, which is now up to $250 million, we will request from them, and they have already made public assurances of their commitments to protect human rights, to protect the rights of women in both transitional and security challenged environments and over the long term, and their openness to working with the international community on a range of issues like that.

We believe this effort, which we support through a number of our partners and through the Office of Transition Initiatives, will be a critical part of helping the Syrian Opposition Council provide services in opposition controlled areas. A large part of this effort is already taking place. There is tight coordination through an organization called the Assistance Coordination Unit of the SOC. And we recognize that our own people and our partners are taking real risks, but are providing significant support in many different ways, specifically in opposition controlled areas.

Senator CORKER. You know, the special investigator inspector that we had in Iraq talked about just recently that he does not see us as any more prepared to do development in similar circumstances today than we were in 2003. That has not worked so well for us. And I wonder if you would just briefly—I want to get on— I know there are other folks who have questions, and I do want to talk to you about USAID Forward and how that affects us dealing with other countries and some of the problems that may exist. I want to talk to you a little bit about some of the trade issues to help countries toward self-sufficiency.

But could you briefly talk to us and give us some assurance that something is different as it relates to how we deliver assistance in places like Syria that are very troubled and obviously have security problems?

Dr. SHAH. Absolutely, Senator. I believe there has been a significant shift in how we do this work. If you look even just in Afghanistan over the last 3 or 4 years, we have more than tripled our civilian presence across the State Department, USAID, and a number of other partners. We have implemented data systems and accountability processes, vetting systems, that have not only established a program to audit 100 percent of locally incurred costs, but with a real rejection rate for, I believe, 21 projects or programs, contracts that were cancelled or not awarded because they failed to pass the vetting system, that is, positives, or hits, that came through the vetting system.

Those are mechanisms that simply did not exist before. They do exist now, and they are highly effective at allowing us to have tighter coordination with our military colleagues, more eyes on effectiveness in our programs, and a more results oriented orientation.

We are seeing the benefits of that today in opposition controlled parts of Syria where more than 65 percent of our humanitarian support goes into those areas through a broad range of partners, and where we are now the primary partner of the Syrian Opposition Council in trying to get everything from generators and fuel to hospitals and facilities, all the way to some form of media and communication and ability for that organization to communicate with its population.

These are capabilities that we have built over the last several years that we did not previously have when the 2003 situation was made reference to.

Senator CORKER. Thank you.

The CHAIRMAN. Thank you.

Senator Cardin.

Senator CARDIN. Thank you, Mr. Chairman. Administrator Shah, first of all, thank you for your leadership. It has been very, very effective in bringing together international development assistance in our security budget, recognizing the returns that we get in our involvement in other countries on our national security front.

I also want to thank you for your commitment to transparency, to gender equity, to dealing with good governance, and dealing with corruption issues to make sure that our aid is actually furthering the stability of a country and not adding to the corruption of certain officials. We have talked about all these issues, and I very much applaud the manner in which you have moved forward in these areas.

Senator Corker has talked about the changes in our Food for Peace Programs. We have a lot of programs that deal with nutrition and food, but perhaps the No. 1 initiative that the Obama administration moved forward with was Feed the Future. So can you just quickly tell us how the reforms that you see in the Food for Peace Program works with the other programs we have, particularly Feed for the Future?

Dr. SHAH. Absolutely. Thank you, Senator, and thank you for your extra investment of time on issues ranging from gender to science, technology, and innovation as we have tried to focus on and accelerate those as core parts of our portfolio. We are very appreciative of that.

With respect to Feed the Future, as I noted, that is intended to be a model program that focuses in 19 countries, many in sub-Saharan Africa, some in Latin America, and south Asia, that are making their own commitments to reform their policies, increase their investments, and move people from a condition of hunger and ongoing need for social support and protection to self-sufficiency and ultimately commercial market success by building their agricultural capabilities.

We have seen incredible success stories from Bangladesh, to Tanzania, to Guatemala, and often those success stories are tied to either new technologies, like deep fertilizer placement in Bangladesh, which has transformed an entire state in that country, to our partnership with Wal-Mart in Guatemala, which is helping tens of thousands of farm households connect to modern international supply chains and improve their livelihoods. That to us is the vision of success.

I visited Guatemala and had a chance to see in the same community where we had a Feed the Future Program, farmers connecting to Wal-Mart and doubling or tripling their incomes. There had been a 35-year Food for Peace Program that provided food to those communities.

What we have been trying to do with that program is shift from giving them bulk grains to giving them high-nutrition foods focusing particularly when kids are in the first 2 years of life where we know nutrition intervention at that point in time has the biggest difference in terms of their livelihoods and their ability to learn and thrive over time. And then connecting those families to these Feed the Future efforts that help them transition from requiring that kind of assistance to being self-sufficient because they are part of a larger effort.

What was tremendous about the Wal-Mart partnership was in that setting, when I asked those families what do you need next— and I thought they would say a new form of agricultural technology or farm implements. Instead, they all said they want schools because now that kids are not working on the farm and they are earning more income, they want to send their kids to school. And that is the path to sustained development that we believe is taking hold in parts of western Guatemala, or southern Tanzania, or eastern Bangladesh, and it is making a huge difference.

Senator CARDIN. Thank you. You mentioned the Office of Science and Technology. You have requested additional funding, for a total of $85 million. Could you just briefly tell us what those additional funds would be used for if it is appropriated by Congress?

Dr. SHAH. Yes, sir. If appropriated, we believe that these investments will help engage our American universities and American businesses and entrepreneurs in helping to bring new scientific and technical breakthroughs to our mission around the world.

This past year, we created what we call the Higher Education Solutions Network with seven universities in the United States. They include development innovation laboratories, such as one at University of California, Berkeley, where students have developed, for example, what they call a cell scope that is an iPhone that connects to a microscope that takes a photo of a blood smear, and can automatically diagnose malaria and potentially TB without requiring going back to a laboratory.

Those kinds of breakthroughs can tremendously change the cost structure of the global health programs that we implement around the world, allowing us to eliminate or eradicate diseases at lower cost. And that is what we are going for. And American technological breakthroughs have been at the core of many of our biggest successes in development around the world.

Senator CARDIN. I think it is very exciting, and I want to just underscore what Senator Corker said. It would be helpful if we had the statutory authority to make sure that, in fact, is done the way that you are suggesting it rather than just rely upon the appropriation process. I think it would be helpful for this committee to weigh in on that initiative, because engaging our private universities, being transformational, and reducing the number of countries requiring direct assistance is exactly what our international development assistance program should do.

One last point on transparency, we have talked about that frequently. And Senator Corker raises the issues of Syria and whether the significant investment that we are making in Syria will get to its intended recipients, and whether the United States will get the benefits of that aid directly as it relates to our security concerns.

There is concern here because we do not control all the terrain on which this aid is going, so I really would appreciate you keeping this committee closely advised as to the accountability and transparency issues as it relates to the funds going into Syria and the help going into Syria so that we have confidence that the significant investments we are making there are fulfilling their purpose.

Thank you, Mr. Chairman.

Dr. SHAH. Thank you, Senator.

The CHAIRMAN. Thank you.

Senator Rubio.

Senator RUBIO. Thank you, and thank you for being here today and for your service to our country.

I wanted to ask you about a program that I think enjoys incredible bipartisan support and has been incredibly effective, and that is PEPFAR, the President's Plan for AIDS Relief. And I am sure you have heard this; I have, from many advocates who are concerned about ongoing cuts to the program that have been phased in over the last few years.

I understand the concept that some of the funds have been moved to the Global Fund and so forth to fight AIDS, and that is worthy as well. But these two programs are synergistic.

I wanted to get your take on truly what is going to be the impact of this continuing reduction of spending on this program, and what it would mean to undermining the goal that the President himself has stated of an AIDS free generation?

Dr. SHAH. Thank you, Senator. The President is very committed to the goal of an AIDS-free generation, and I appreciate your advocacy and leadership on this issue as well.

America has played a unique role in starting and helping to accelerate the fight against HIV/AIDS, and today the United States spends more than $8 billion a year in global health, the majority of which is focused on our efforts to control and reverse the trends around HIV/AIDS. It is by far the largest category of our foreign assistance and the largest single item within the entire 150 Account budget.

With respect to PEPFAR specifically, the President's fiscal year 2014 request includes $1.65 billion for the Global Fund. This is an important year. The Global Fund has been through a tremendous restructuring, and through that restructuring, they are going to be working very closely with our bilateral program. And we see the Global Fund as a mechanism to accelerate other donors' commitments to maintain and accelerate this fight.

I would say with respect, I think in the countries where we work, we are seeing more, not less, resources go to HIV/AIDS control and treatment. In South Africa, as we modulate our own investment, the government is more than making up for gaps, and, in fact, that transition is one that has been carefully negotiated with them and one they are eager to pursue. So they have ownership and responsibility for what I believe is the more than 4 million South African AIDS patients, some of which I have had a chance to meet and that are partners, and we proudly work to serve.

So our goal is to reach 15 million global AIDS patients on treatment. That is a global number that we have all agreed to. I believe the current global effort is at 8 billion. And the way we believe we will get there is by crowding in investments from, first, the countries in which we work, second, other donors and other partners, and, third, by maintaining very strong American budgets for global health and HIV/AIDS.

Senator RUBIO. So just the takeaway then is that even though our investment into PEPFAR particularly has eroded over the last few years, the difference is being made up by local countries' own investment in these programs, and that that will more than adequate to continue to meet the benchmarks that we have set?

Dr. SHAH. Absolutely. In fact, we have accelerated and have met every benchmark we have set earlier than the time indicates. And I think that will continue to be the case through this second term.

Senator RUBIO. So you are confident in saying that this reduction in spending on PEPFAR will not lead to erosion in the gains that have been made and in the progress that is being made?

Dr. SHAH. Absolutely not. In fact, I am confident that our approach of bringing together our global health investments around the world and bringing other partners to do more will actually accelerate impacts. We genuinely believe we will see twice as many AIDs patients, supported by the global partnership, not just the United States. And we are absolutely committed to and very confident that we will achieve an AIDS-free generation largely by targeting pregnant women with antiretroviral therapy, early testing, and diagnostics.

Senator RUBIO. OK. Just to another part of the world quickly, and it is an article that came out on March 4 and talked about, "Dam and Other Afghanistan Projects Being Scaled Back as United States Picks Up Its Pace of Withdrawal." The concern is that the United States is investing a tremendous amount of treasure and obviously lives and blood and otherwise in this region, and scores of people have lost their lives to secure, for example, this area around Kajaki Dam in southern Afghanistan so that the USAID could safely manage a major construction project.

But now it appears that we have decided not to complete the project, and instead leave it to an Afghan electricity company that our own special inspector general has criticized for lacking the necessary expertise.

Obviously the decision to move from Afghanistan is one that enjoys popular support, and it is a decision that is not in your agency per se. But can you talk about the impacts of these projects that we have invested so much money in, that now we are either turning over to Afghan institutions that are documented as having very little accountability, unless you disagree, and then we can talk about that. But more importantly, there is this notion that these major projects that we are on the verge of completing or what have you and have already invested a lot of money in, we are either not going to complete and turn it to others to do or not do at all because of the eroding security situation in some of these regions, and the challenge that that poses.

Dr. SHAH. Well, I thank you for the question, and I would note also that American investment in Afghanistan has already allowed for a more than tripling of energy access for Afghan citizens, including in Kandahar City, which is what the Kajaki Dam is intended to improve upon.

We saw that article, and it inaccurately reflected a sense that we were cutting back or scaling back our commitments there. In fact, I just spoke with General Dunford earlier this week who spoke specifically about his recent visit to Kajaki where the USAID military partnership to refurbish and expand its capacity to produce electricity is proceeding at pace. We think we will be successful.

The partnership is with Black & Veatch/Louis Berger, which is a firm that has been doing the project. And it is also with the Afghan Electricity Company. The reason they are part of the partnership is they have to ultimately collect the revenue to sustain that effort, and we have been working with them, in some cases using new technology, like mobile-phone-based electricity payments, which has allowed them to increase by more than 300 percent their revenue collection from Afghans who benefit from this electricity.

And that is what will be required to sustain these efforts over time, so we do have to work in a responsible, transparent way with our Afghan partners. I think that is a good example of how we believe we can be successful. And Kajaki remains a priority within our shared military-civilian campaign plan there.

The CHAIRMAN. Thank you.

Senator Kaine.

Senator KAINE. Dr. Shah, great to be with you today.

When the President in his State of the Union talked about the big goal, the eradication of extreme poverty in the world over two decades, the United States in tandem with others, you know, I applauded because I love the big goals, and I think we are sent here to do big things, and we ought to be looking for the big goals. But at the same time, I find myself wondering a little bit.

Sometimes there is a hubris that we have if something goes wrong in Syria or North Korea, and we kind of get into what did we do wrong, or what is our responsibility. And as I read some of the development literature about why the bottom billion or the bottom million, you know, the United States not doing enough usually is not one of the reasons why cultures or people get locked into extreme poverty. So clearly, a goal like that of extreme poverty eradication in two decades is one that has to be done in partnership, and it also has to be one around which there are some pretty clear metrics.

I just would like it if we have talked about this in Senator Cardin's office, a little bit about hunger and preventable child death. But let us talk sort of about metrics, and let us talk about partnerships that you intend to leverage, both NGO partnerships, but also, you know, how are we incorporating other nations into this goal?

Dr. SHAH. Well, thank you, Senator, and thank you for your extra commitment to this particular issue because I think it is an issue where real significant political leadership will, in fact, make a huge difference.

The President claimed and put forward the goal of ending extreme poverty within two decades because we believe for the first time in human history that it is achievable. We have seen between 2005 and 2008, for the very first time in our history, extreme dollar and a quarter a day poverty fall in every region of the world for the first time. And we believe we are on that path today. We know that there are about 1.2 billion people that live in that sort of excruciatingly difficult situation, and we know that bringing them into a more connected global economy will be the path that gets them out of extreme poverty.

So the question then, as you point out, becomes, what are the right metrics to measure? We believe the dual goals of ending hunger and ending preventable child death are the areas where America can make the biggest contribution toward that outcome specifically. We measure our efforts in food and hunger by looking at incomes of farm households, by looking at the number of farm households we reach, by looking at agricultural development and agricultural GDP growth specifically in countries where we focus, and then by correlating that to reductions in extreme poverty.

We know agricultural GDP growth is three to six times more likely to reduce extreme poverty, and we have seen that trend play out in the 19 Feed the Future countries that have had on average a 5.6-percent annualized reduction since joining the program.

On child death and on global health in particular, we can measure a number of specific things, but under-5 child mortality is the core measure of how many children are dying. And it is actually a pretty good correlate for other morbidity related measures about disease and loss of productivity related to child death, meaning if a lot of kids die, then a lot of kids are also getting sick and not going to school and other negative consequences.

So those are the two things. We measure them. You can actually download an iPhone app that we have that shows you the health statistics and under-5 mortality statistics elsewhere.

Going forward, as part of achieving this goal, we will also expand our efforts in energy access because that is such an important driver of helping families move out of poverty, and believe it is possible to double energy access in sub-Saharan Africa from 30 to roughly 60 percent, and to achieve that in a very highly leveraged way with strong partnerships with American businesses that help bring energy to many parts of the world.

So we believe that these objectives are possible, but they are only possible with setting a big goal, bringing other countries and international institutions to bear. The United Nations will in the next 18 months identify a new set of global millennium development goals, and John Podesta is our representative to that process and has also advocated for setting the goal of ending extreme poverty within two decades.

And quite frankly, the United States makes outsized and critically important investments in those places where extreme poverty will be concentrated 4 or 5, 6 years from now, places like Afghanistan, Pakistan, Somalia, and with a results-oriented public-private partnership approach, we believe it is achievable.

Senator KAINE. The public-private partnership approach, the data I see suggests now, you know, foreign aid dollars, if you look at a public-private, 10 to 15 percent is public, and 80 to 85 percent is private—philanthropic, NGO. Talk a little bit about the leveraging you do in tackling a big challenge like this with the NGO community.

Dr. SHAH. Absolutely, and, in fact, that is the exact opposite from 40 years ago. Forty years ago, flows into these countries were largely public investments, and private investments were the 15 percent. Now that has been flipped on its head, and that is why we have pursued USAID Forward as a reform agenda that allows us to partner differently with companies all around the world. When we engage, for example, in ending preventable child death in India, we are not spending more money in India by any stretch, but we are working with Unilever and other partners that can get improved technologies and start businesses that reach some communities that can be profitable businesses, and also can work toward the objective of saving children's lives and ending extreme poverty.

And that increasingly is defining a broad range of partnerships. USAID has been recognized by its peers as leading in this area, and we have now completed almost 1,100 of these public-private partnerships around the world, many of which I think are a genuine model of how we can achieve the end of extreme poverty.

Senator KAINE. Great. Thank you.

The CHAIRMAN. Thank you.

Administrator, let me just follow up a moment on Syria before I go to one area of concern that I have in the budget. Have you been approached or has there been any discussion in any interagency process about the need to achieve credit with the Syrian people for our assistance, balancing obviously protecting our aid provided by not marking everything so that it says U.S.—delivered by the people of the United States, but still trying to develop some foundation of having them understand who is being supportive here.

Has there been any talk about changing the current approach, going primarily through the United Nations and possibly filtering some of this assistance through the opposition that we have vetted as opposition that we believe share our values?

Dr. SHAH. Yes, Senator; there have been precisely those conversations. I would note that of the $385 million of humanitarian assistance that we provide, we use the United Nations as core partners in delivering that assistance, but also a sizable proportion goes to NGOs and other private organizations that are able to sometimes more effectively and with U.S. branding reach opposition controlled areas and settings. And we believe more than 60 to 65 percent of our aid and assistance actually goes into opposition controlled areas and targets specifically those communities. And we make every effort to not only brand and publicize when we can and when that is safe, but we also have in parallel, TV and media efforts to try to communicate what the United States is doing.

In addition to that, on the services side, we are working directly with the Syrian Opposition Council to help them provide that support and do this together, and that was the additional $250 million that Secretary Kerry announced this weekend that is separate and apart from the basic humanitarian aid, but often will provide water services, or diesel generators and fuel, or other things that are critically needed essential services, as an economy is going through that very difficult time.

I would say one last thing about this, sir, is the extent to which we believe there has been specific targeting by the Assad regime of our humanitarian partners. We know there have been 143 deaths of doctors and nurses and other medical personnel that have worked with and at our various supported field hospitals or hospital sites. We know that more than eight U.N. international staff have been killed as part of efforts to provide services. We have very clear data that bakeries and hospitals are preferentially targeted by regime forces in opposition controlled areas, for example, in parts of Aleppo.

The safety and security concerns are very real, and we do respect our partners, some of whom are working with Syrian-American doctors, for example, that do some extraordinarily courageous things, but they do it with a real concern for their own safety.

The CHAIRMAN. Well, I am not surprised about Assad, and I am concerned, having seen the most recent reports about chemical weapon usage, if that is verified, it makes all the more case that we have to change our dynamics there and the tipping point.

Let me go to an area of the world that I am confounded by the administration as well as previous administrations' views. We have seen a continuing significant decline in our assistance to the Western Hemisphere, particularly to Latin America and the Caribbean. And I am amazed because all the things that we debate here in the—or many of the things, I should say, not all the things, but many of the things we debate here in the Congress are, in fact, emanating in our front yard.

If I do not want to see undocumented immigration in this country, there are push factors—people leave their countries for only two reasons: civil unrest or dire economic circumstances. Otherwise they would stay. So it is in our interest through our development programs to try create greater economic growth in our own hemisphere.

If we want to help governments stop transnational crime and narcotics trafficking, you have to give poor growers who have to sustain their families, alternative crops so that they are not growing coca at the end of the day. That is in our national interest because the last thing we want to see is those narcotics end up in the streets of our cities.

If you want to open up greater markets for U.S. products and services for which there is an affinity by Latin Americans to U.S. products and services, you want to create economies that are ultimately going to buy more U.S. products and services. If you want to look at some of the incredibly important biodiversity issues that affect us collectively, you want to think about how you change the dynamics of eviscerating a rain forest. If you want to stop some of the diseases that had been largely eradicated and now begin to rise again, such as tuberculosis, they know no boundaries.

So I am amazed that with all of those realities and with the unrest and the movement away from democracy in the region toward dictatorships and totalitarianism, that we continue to cut—this is like a 6-percent cut, but if you compound it over the last several years, you are looking at a very enormous cut. And we just finished talking about poverty. Well, about 30 percent of all of the region's population is below the poverty level, and of those, 66 million are in extreme poverty. This is in our own neighborhood.

So I do not understand the cuts that we are seeing. I know that we are going through programmatic changes with Mexico and Colombia. We are moving away from hardware to institution-building. But when I look at the totality of these cuts, I just do not get it, and that is why we create a void in which people like Chavez when he was alive ultimately filled the void, where the Chinese are coming in our own hemisphere, where the Iranians have been promoting diplomacy in the hemisphere. I just do not get it.

So I look at that. I look at in another context—a cut on Cuba's democracy program at a time in which, in fact, we had 6,000 arrests and detentions last year. We had the Ladies in White, a group of women whose husbands or sons sit in Castro's jail simply because they sought peaceful change in their country, get attacked brutally every week. We saw Oswaldo Payá assassinated, one of the leading human rights individuals inside of Cuba. His daughter was here not too long ago and made it very clear to us, from all the information, that he was assassinated. And yet we see a cut in that program.

So I look at the totality of this, and it certainly does not make public policy sense to me. So I am going to be looking to try to change this because I just think we have created—and it is not until we have a major problem in the hemisphere that everybody will run, and we will spend a fortune instead of doing the right thing now that can ultimately create the seeds of democracy in open markets within the hemisphere.

If there is one bright spot here, it is CARSI, which obviously is one of my critical concerns, and I will be traveling on the break to this region, in terms of preventing violence, combating narcotics trafficking, increasing citizen security. And I look forward to hearing how you are going to use the funding for 2014 there, as well as how do we create in these countries fiscal and policy reforms that can sustain us moving forward.

So, I have gone over my time, but this is one of my passions and no one else seems to have a greater passion for it. But it just does not make a lot of sense in my mind in terms of the national interests and security of the United States.

Dr. SHAH. Thank you, Senator. We had the chance to discuss this, and I very much appreciate and recognize your strong and consistent leadership here. We, too, believe the region is critical and important. We have had to present a budget that conforms to an overall 6-percent reduction, which has forced a lot of difficult tradeoffs at a time when the actual number of humanitarian disasters around the world is doubling what we need to respond to in terms of case loads.

There have been, as you point out, some critical areas, like CARSI, where we are presenting in this budget a 23-percent increase in our investment and our focus on that critical security program for the Northern Triangle. We know that our efforts have been delivering real results. In Mexico, where we have worked on prosecution-related partnerships, we have seen the rates in participating cities go up significantly and delays go down significantly. We built a new partnership with Los Angeles to bring some of the crime control measures that have been effective and proven in that setting to other countries in the region. We know that the alternative crop program, to which you made reference, in Peru has been successful there and a model for work in other parts of the world.

And we also see across regions—Latin America has been by far the most successful with public-private partnerships. For every dollar we put into a public-private partnership in that region, we are able to attract $2.53 dollars from private sector, local partners. And we believe that that serves as an engine of sustaining significant development, investment, and partnership.

But we recognize that this is a very important region, and we have had to make tough tradeoffs in a budget that we certainly wish was larger.

The CHAIRMAN. I will just close on this, Administrator. For several years now, whether you were the Administrator or previous ones, I have heard that there are always tough tradeoffs. And where the tough tradeoff goes always is Latin America and the Caribbean. That is always where it ends up being cut. And I just think that that is foolish at the end of the day. We are going to have a problem, and then when we have the problem, we will spend a fortune.

We did the same thing with Central American wars, and then after we spent a fortune in Central America providing democracy, we got out, and we did not lay the foundation of the seeds that would have provided long-term growth and prosperity.

Senator Corker.

Senator CORKER. Thank you, Mr. Chairman. I am glad to hear you talk about a topic you care deeply about. Thank you.

Mr. Administrator, I want to talk to you this round of questions about USAID Forward. And, again, I want to say I really appreciate the thrust that you have had toward self-sufficiency. I know what you are trying to do is move away from NGOs that are not necessarily based in the area or based in the country, and try to build capacity with governments that are there.

And obviously, you know, foreign aid is under criticism right now. A lot of people here in our country see needs here and wonder why we are doing things in other places, and so I do think that the move toward self-sufficiency is a good one. On the other hand, dealing in that manner can create a lot of political risk. You end up dealing with governments that sometimes commit fraud and are involved in corruption. It does mean probably that we move toward more direct involvement with them.

And I just wondered if you might talk a little bit about your concerns there and your plans to alleviate those, and also comment on whether—if you were moving ahead with this effort, which I hope you will, if you see countries where corruption and other kinds of things are taking place—you will withdraw due to their lack of accountability and responsibility.

Dr. SHAH. Thank you, Senator, and I appreciate the opportunity to discuss with you USAID Forward. This has been our signature agency reform effort and has covered three major areas of transformation. One is how we partner around the world to which you have asked that question.

But there have been other areas of focus within USAID Forward as well, a real focus on science, technology, and innovation, and making sure we bring the best of what America has to offer to our work has been a core element, as well as an absolute focus on measurement, results, evaluation, and transparency, which has been an important part of this.

But going to your question specifically, a core part of our thinking is using and partnering with those who represent real local solutions. We can bring the cost structure of our work down and create the kind of institutional strength that can sustain these efforts and activities after American aid and assistance goes away. And that is the basic theory.

Nearly every one of our peer countries spends somewhere between 60 and 80 percent of their total budget on these types of local institutions. When I started at USAID, we spent 9 percent in that space. So we have had a focused effort to increase that percentage to something that we think is responsible, and we have asked every mission to identify what that responsible level might be, taking in account for all kinds of considerations, including corruption and weak institutions locally.

The result of this has been a process where we have moved more resources to local partners. But in all of those cases, we have conducted careful and rigorous country assessments. If we are going to work with a local government, we assess their capacity to be transparent. If they are not, we say, sorry, we cannot work with you. And in some cases, they will come back and say, OK, well, what can we do differently as they have in Malawi and Liberia, where, as a result of receiving our assessments, they said, OK, we will embed an international auditing operation within our Ministry of Finance, or we will build a strong public financial management system that gives you the confidence. And then, by the way, you can work with us, and then other partners can also work with us because we are committed to fighting corruption as best we can with your partnership.

So I believe this effort has really transformed our capabilities. Our staff is out and about working with partners. We are able to find and support local entrepreneurs. We have offered credit guarantees to dozens of local banks that have increased their lending to small and medium enterprises in Africa, for example, by $530 million last year, at almost no expense to us because those credit guarantees do not get called down because the people tend to be good for the loans.

And we have seen external validation from nearly every major development entity and expert organization in this town, ranging from AEI and Heritage to the Center for American Progress and OXFAM.

So, I know that this is tough. I know in places like Afghanistan where corruption can be a very significant endemic challenge we have a different approach.

In that setting, most of our ''on budget assistance'' goes to an entity called the Afghan Reconstruction Trust Fund, which is managed and operated by the World Bank. And while that is not quite what we meant by local solutions, it protects and safeguards very significant American investment in that country's future, and we will not take undue risks in that context.

Senator CORKER. Well, again, I like the thrust that you have with ag. I like the thrust that you have with USAID Forward. I think the movement toward self-sufficiency and dealing with people in their own countries is a great—I like the way you are levering PEPFAR, the way you discussed with Senator Rubio.

One area that I think we are not doing a good job in leveraging is in trade. In other words, if we want some of these developing countries to really move toward self-sufficiency, something we can do well is really increase the ability of those countries to trade internationally and to trade with us. And yet if we look at the efforts, there is really not a coordinated effort. GAO says there is 18 different agencies that focus on trade. We understand when the report comes out each year to focus on how much effort toward

trade is taking place, people just start lumping in things: a road-
way in Afghanistan, something else.

I am wondering if you might consider putting some effort into a
coordinated trade effort so that we can help leverage many of the
self-sufficiencies you are talking about and move away from the
day-to-day assistance effort that we continue to be involved in.

Dr. SHAH. Well, thank you, Senator. The short answer, sir, is
absolutely we will. And I believe in this second term, in particular,
this will be an increased focus, specifically with respect to some of
our efforts in Africa, but also in context ranging from Jordan to
Afghanistan to Haiti. In fact, in Afghanistan, one of the most important things we can do is help clean up the process by which customs are collected and revenues are generated and then actually
sent back to the government. And by cleaning up that process, we
think they can significantly improve their domestic revenue collection, which will be critical to smoothing the reality of less international expenditure in that country.

In Jordan, we have seen a 250-percent improvement in customs
collections because of our partnerships with them. Sometimes it is
bringing technology to border posts. Sometimes it is just bringing
transparency to those settings and helping to improve transparent
customs collection.

In parts of east Africa, as coordinated with our Feed the Future
effort, we are actively expanding the focus on regional trade. In
Tanzania, for example, as a precondition for being part of our partnership, we asked the Tanzanians to forgo the export bans they
have put on Tanzanian agriculture. Every time food prices go up
or there is a regional shortage, they use those export bans. And
that, of course, creates a strong disincentive for investment. So
they have made that commitment, and now we are working with
them to clean up the kind of checkpoint process as roads cross from
one country into neighboring countries. The same is true of South
Sudan and its neighbors.

So these types of efforts, while they do not get a lot of publicity
and do not tug at the heartstrings in the same way, they do, in
fact, improve domestic revenue collection speed, local and regional
trade and investment, and are often very high on the list of what
local businesses will ask us to advocate for and prioritize. And you
are absolutely right, and we should do more, and we will try to.

The CHAIRMAN. Senator Casey. On the second round, I go to
members who have not had an opportunity.

Senator CASEY. I am very happy about that. [Laughter.]

Mr. Chairman, we often say thank you, Mr. Chairman. I want
to say it loud and clear. Thank you, Mr. Chairman. We know of the
seniority rule.

I wanted to, first, by way of commendation for the work that you
have done. We appreciate that. You have been stellar in a very difficult environment and in a very tough position.

I wanted to direct your attention to two areas. One is the question of food aid. Too often around here, and I point a finger of
blame at myself and probably could extend that to others as well.
But we do not talk enough about the impact of the international
affairs budget on our States and on the country, in addition to

making the argument about security and the important necessity of food aid and aid like that.

Interestly, in Pennsylvania, three numbers: 3, 223, and 112. Just looking at these numbers today, and we should have them—I should have them memorized by now. The U.S. Export-Import Bank financed over $3 billion in exports from 223 companies in 112 communities in Pennsylvania. We do not say that enough. We do not often make that very important and substantial and measurable nexus between that support and what happens in a State like Pennsylvania.

We have more than 30,000 international students studying in Pennsylvania in 2011, and they brought over $950 million into the State's economy. So all these subjects we are talking about when it comes to this budget are significant for our States and for the country.

First of all, with regard to food aid, I was struck by—and I am sorry I missed your testimony and your personal testimony, or the testimony you gave today. But I was noting in your prepared testimony, and you may have gotten to this already, but I think it bears repeating, that you assert on page 4 that pursuant to this year's budget request, it would "enable us to feed 2 to 4 million more hungry men, women, and children every year with the same resources." You go on to talk about buying food locally can speed the arrival of aid by as much as 14 weeks.

It can also cost much less. And you go on from there to make the case on flexibility.

I guess I would focus the first question on how do you make that happen? How do you ensure that the potential recipients of this aid get not just get the kind of food, but in particular, the nutritious foods that they need, even if they cannot be bought in local markets?

Dr. SHAH. Well, thank you, Senator, and thank you for your unique leadership on food and hunger issues at home and around the world. The legislation that you have worked on is often referenced appropriately as the underpinning of our Feed the Future initiative and program. And your leadership on thinking through food aid is very important to our aspiration to get this done.

Senator CASEY. Thank you.

Dr. SHAH. The reality is that over the last 3 years we have an actual database driven by the fact that we have had in the international disaster assistance account about $300 million a year for a program called Local and Regional Procurement. That program provides us with real data about where we have been buying food, how long it takes us to take regionally procured food to children and women in needy situations.

It has shown us that we can use new and different kinds of tools ranging from local foods and new food formulations to vouchers and other card-based systems that empower people in settings where we cannot physically reach them with food convoys for security reasons. And it has given us the confidence that we can use the teams and the organizations we have in place to implement this approach in a way that delivers real measurable results.

And I would also add that through that effort, we know that when we buy food locally, we put it in a bag that says "USAID from the American People,'' and it has the same brand value as anything else. In fact, I have actually been in settings where we are feeding children with high nutrition pastes and things like that. And I can assure you they are well aware because each packet is individually wrapped and labeled and branded, that those benefits accrue to them because of American commitment, generosity, and humanitarian support.

So we have a strong database that indicates that this kind of flexibility will reach the 4 million additional children. And we know that, frankly, this year, the Syria crisis is so dramatic and significant that all of our flexibility will be absorbed in that setting, requiring us to move children in Somalia, DRC, and Pakistan from the LRP program to the Title II program. And because of the efficiency differences, we will end up moving hundreds of thousands of kids off the support programs as we make that transition if we do not do this reform.

Senator CASEY. I appreciate that, and I have limited time, but I will just raise one more question. You can amplify the answer in written form as well. But on Syria, I know you have been asked a number of questions today, and I am sorry I was not here for that.

But I think we are still struggling with the best approach, and I think it is both a bipartisan struggle, but also a bipartisan effort that is being undertaken. Senator Rubio and I have legislation. Senator Coons and several others are working with us on it. But we are trying to move forward in a way that would be constructive and effective in bringing the conflict to an end and to be able to deal with the aftermath.

And I know this may be by way of reiteration, but just maybe a couple of words about how you are going to continue to make sure that the food aid gets to folks either on the Syrian side or the refugee side in places like Turkey?

Dr. SHAH. Well, thank you. On the humanitarian side, we have provided at this point nearly $400 million of humanitarian support. We know that we are reaching 2.4 million Syrians inside of Syria with everything from food to clean water to earlier in the season winterization kits and blankets for their homes and their living situations. And we know that we are providing through a range of partners support to the 1½ million refugees with a real focus on those in Jordan and Turkey.

In addition, we have also provided actual direct support to Jordan to help them absorb what is essentially 42,000 children who are now joining the Jordanian public school system in the neighborhoods along the Syrian border and placing extraordinary strains on their domestic situation. It has been difficult. Access inside Syria is the biggest challenge, but we work with a range of partners, including NGOs, that can focus and work in opposition controlled areas.

In addition to that, Secretary Kerry this past weekend noted an additional $250 million commitment specifically to the Syrian Opposition Council to support services and governance efforts in opposition controlled areas. And we are coordinating an international effort to bolster the SOCs capacity to provide real services and governance in certain parts of opposition controlled Syria. And

as Secretary Kerry noted, in making that announcement the Syrian
opposition has worked with us to also make commitments to respect women's rights, gender considerations, and to promote openness in their approach to governance as this gets off the ground.

So we are doing everything we can. It is a very difficult operating
environment as, of course, you are well aware. And our people take
real risks to do this, but it is in our national security interests to
be actively engaged here.

Senator CASEY. Thanks very much.

The CHAIRMAN. Senator Rubio.

Senator RUBIO. Thank you. And the chairman brought this up
earlier, but I wanted to close the loop and just add my own
thoughts on the Cuban democracy programming. And he may have
made this point, and so I apologize. I was in the back for a few
moments.

But my understanding is that your core budget at USAID has
taken about a 10-percent reduction, is that correct? But the Cuban
democracy programs have taken a 25-percent reduction, which
seems way out of proportion to the general reduction for a program
of this small scale.

And a couple of points come to mind. No. 1 is, every time some
of our colleagues or others visit Cuba, one of the first things they
get complaints about from the Castro government is the democracy
programs. They absolutely hate it. That is No. 1. And there is a
reason for that, because not only are they antidemocratic, but
apparently they felt these programs in the past have been quite
effective.

The second problem then is, over the last few years, and this is
documented. I am not making this up. Some of our colleagues, including the former chairman of this committee through staff, held
this program up with endless questions about it. And so I do not
think it is a coincidence that this reduced so completely out of proportion from the size and scope of the program. And I just hope
that this will be reversed because I think it is a terrible precedent
and a terrible idea.

Beyond that, I do have concerns that I hope will be addressed
when the funding does come out, and hopefully it will be at a
higher level once it goes through this process, that it is truly being
purposed for democracy purposes. And I have no problem, and obviously I do not have anything here to say today about the people
who are currently receiving the funds and how they are using it.
I just think it is important that we be clear, this is a democracy
program, and there are actually provisions in law—the Cuban
Democracy Act, the Lever Debt Act—that actually condition what
it can be spent on and what it cannot be spent on.

So I am not claiming that it is being spent on things that it
should not be. I think it is very important that we be clear that
this money is being spent on the promotion of democracy, not on
the creation of grassroots community organizations that specialize
in, you know, better sewage treatment programs or what have you.
This is about democracy. That is what this program is about. And
I hope we will be vigilant in that regard.

And I also think it is important to ask ourselves—and by the
way, this is not a 1-year cut. My understanding, Mr. Chairman, is

this has been a steady erosion of this program over the last few years. But a 25-percent cut on such a small program, combined with we have seen some of the political resistance to it over the last few years. I personally do not believe it is a coincidence, and I hope that this can be reversed.

On a broader point about foreign aid in particular, in general, and I would use Egypt as an example, in particular.

I am a believer in foreign aid. I think it is an important part of our foreign policy. It gives us influence. It allows us to impact events around the world. I think it is an important tool in furthering our national interest. And I am sure you agree—I know you agree—that the primary purpose of foreign aid is to further our national interests.

Americans are concerned, however, when they see foreign aid going into places—and I would just use Egypt as an example—where you have government leaders and others in that society that are participating not just antidemocratic things, but just systematically violating the rights of religious minorities and others. And I think my question is on a broader scale—I am a firm believer, and I want to get your thoughts—that our foreign aid should be conditioned, and increasingly conditioned, on our national interests and on our values, particularly when it comes to foreign aid along the lines of supporting governments and their economic programs.

And I just think it is critically important that our foreign aid come with strings—quite frankly, not with strings, with ropes attached, that ensure that the money is being used to further our national interests. It is not a charity. It is not paying tribute to a foreign government the way one leading cleric in Egypt classified it as. It is something that is designed to further our national interests and our values.

And I just want your general thoughts about what we can do to improve on that front. What can we do to ensure that our foreign aid is a carrot, and, quite frankly, an incentive for governments to move their societies and their economy in a direction that is good for them, but ultimately is really good for us because it is our money.

Dr. SHAH. Well, thank you, Senator. On both points, I can assure you on Cuba, your point is well taken, and we will make sure as we have done that the focus of this program sticks to the letter of the law and is focused on democracy and civil society. And per the recent GAO report, I think those third party assessments show that, in fact, that has been how we have managed to implement this effort.

With respect to the general point about foreign aid, I am in complete agreement that our foreign assistance advances our national interests. Sometimes it advances our national interests by seeking and achieving commitments to certain types of reforms that can range from sectorial policy reforms to larger scale commitments to protect the rights of women and minorities in certain situations.

We would be eager to work with you to articulate different forms of conditionality, but Egypt is a good example because over the last year and a half, as we have reshaped the program in Egypt, we have essentially focused on a handful of priorities. The first is the macroeconomic situation, and we have, in fact, conditioned our cash transfers and loan guarantee support efforts to Egyptian participation and negotiations in the IMF program, because that is what is required for them to be successful.

Second, we focus very much on youth employment. As Secretary Kerry recently said, that is the core challenge, and we know that our efforts help open up the economy, have led to 3,700 small business starts; 7.9 million loans to local small-scale businesses that create jobs for young people in those settings.

Third, we focus very much on women and minorities. We specifically support the Coptic Evangelical Organization for social services, and a range of other minority rights organizations, and have conditioned as part of our diplomatic dialogue this assistance on ensuring space remains open for those civil organizations in respect of those rights.

Senator RUBIO. I am sorry, when you say "diplomatic dialogue," we have told them we want you to protect the Coptic Christians, or we have actually said——

Dr. SHAH. In every conversation, absolutely.

Senator RUBIO. All right.

Dr. SHAH. And, we do not link everything to precise conditionality, but the basic themes of supporting the macropackage with the IMF, supporting women and minorities, ensuring rights and open space for civil society, and allowing private enterprise to flourish and create jobs in areas where there is a lot of young unemployment have been the drivers of our dialogue and are the basic conditions for this program being in place.

The CHAIRMAN. Thank you.

Senator Coons.

Senator COONS. Thank you. I want to thank Senator Menendez for convening this critically important hearing.

And I want to applaud you, Administrator Shah, for your determination, your vision, your leadership, and your deep commitment to development issues. I share the views expressed by several of my colleagues that development is absolutely essential to America's national interests, and I intend to continue to work with you to ensure strong support for the appropriate balance between diplomacy, defense, and development.

But in order for me to be true to the concerns of my home State, we also need to continue to pursue efficiencies to make sure that funds that are being spent on foreign assistance are spent wisely and well. And I have been impressed with your innovative approach to furthering our development goals, to insisting on accountability and to transparency. And so let me dive into a couple of things around it if I might.

I also want to commend the work of this committee in partnership with USAID on Syria and Syrian relief, and I commend Secretary Kerry's significant increase and support through the SOC, something we have discussed before and you know I have pressed for.

Africa trade hubs, if I might first. I have been impressed with the work of USAID's regional trade hubs that help build regional capacity in Africa and create economic opportunity for Americans and Africans. How can they be expanded to promote and further interregional trade, and what ways do you think USAID can contribute to expanded opportunities for trade investment in Africa?

Dr. SHAH. Well, thank you, Senator, and thank you for your ongoing support of this agenda and your tremendous personal experience and guidance on a range of issues as we go forward.

Specifically with respect to the African trade hubs, I would point out that in both west Africa, eastern Africa, and southern Africa, we have had independent evaluations that demonstrate that over the period of 7 to 10 years, these trade hubs have significantly improved interregional trade, that countries depend on them for having clear and transparent custom systems and the ability to move goods across borders.

We are implementing reforms as we speak. We are tying these very closely to our agricultural programs and agricultural trade efforts, and that has already borne quite a lot of fruit. The second way we are informing them by is linking these to some of the efforts to fight corruption and improve transparency with customs, collection, and informal collections of tariffs at border posts. And a third has been tying the trade hubs to our efforts to expand access to energy in the region. Many of these settings—energy, trade—will be one of the next big areas of regional trade and expansion.

So we are pursuing all of those with respect to these trade hubs and obviously maintaining the budget support for these efforts has been a challenge, but we think there is strong external validation for the effectiveness of these efforts.

Senator COONS. Well, they are a modest investment that I think has seen some real outcomes. I look forward to working with you on those. There are so many other things I would like to talk about: the Higher Education Solutions Network, which I think is a tremendous idea, your, I think, bold reform, USAID Forward.

But let me also talk about food aid reform, which is a significant proposal in this year's budget. If you would, please discuss the reforms to the Food for Peace Program that were included in the Senate version of last year's farm bill, what benefits they would bring to the program, and what the proposals are in the administration's budget, and how that would deal with inefficiencies in the current system. As I know, it has already been discussed, but continue to protect the vital interests of American farmers and shippers as well. How does it strike the right balance?

Dr. SHAH. Well, thank you. We believe this proposal does, in fact, strike the right balance. It incorporates many of the components of what the Senate bill was moving toward, which is giving us more flexibility to use and purchase food locally and to do that when it is cheaper, more effective, it does not compete with American-produced commodities, and it can help save lives in emergency settings.

And we have a strong database over the last several years of examples where we have done precisely that. And we also have a strong database that shows that recipients of that type of aid and assistance have the same appreciation of it as coming from the United States and being branded as such as in the traditional programs.

I would add that this proposal includes a commitment to continue to buy the majority of food from American producers and shipped on American-flag vessels. But we want to do that in a more modern and science-based way. The science tells us that traditional commodity gifts are less useful at saving children's lives at times of crisis than high nutrition, micronutrient enhanced, prepackaged foods that are now being developed in Europe and elsewhere in the world. We think they should be developed in the United States. We have the best agricultural system and the best agricultural companies on the planet, and we should be at the forefront of that.

So our team has created a pipeline of 10 to 12 new products and technologies that will be emerging with those types of products. We think that is very much the future of a science-based aid program that can save the most lives at times of crises, and we think that will be very effective.

Finally, I will just say with respect to shipping that we have looked very carefully at this and provided a support program expansion for the Department of Transportation. We believe that most—in fact, there is quite a lot of concentration in this industry with our use of a few firms really being at issue here, and we have designed that to be able to ensure that those partners have a transition path in which they receive support and can maintain American jobs. And that was the purpose of that part of the proposal.

Senator COONS. I look forward to working with you on a number of these different great challenges of development. I have additional questions I would love to ask on Kenya and the Democratic Republic of the Congo that I will submit for the record.

Thank you, Mr. Chairman, for the chance to question today.

The CHAIRMAN. Thank you, Senator Coons.

Senator Murphy.

Senator MURPHY. Thank you, Mr. Chairman. Welcome, Administrator Shah. Thank you very much for joining us. Let me just associate myself with the comments of Senator Coons and others. We are so appreciative of your work, and I think we understand now more than ever that this Nation does not remain secure unless we have a commitment to foreign aid and an understanding that the only way to win the argument as we have been talking about on this committee week after week and month after month is to make sure that we are a true partner for development.

Administrator Shah, I wanted to talk about recent events in Russia for a few moments. I do not know if that has come up yet, but we certainly were very disappointed to see the new Russian disposition not only on USAID, but also on other American NGOs that have been very good work there.

And it is an open-ended question for you to just give the committee an update as to our strategy vis-a-vis Russia going forward. To the extent that we do not have a physical presence there of USAID, can we still accomplish with respect to our development goals there from outside the country, and what do you see as our future disposition toward that nation, and is there anything left that we can continue to do without a presence there?

Dr. SHAH. Thank you, Senator, and thanks for raising that particular issue. It has not yet come up.

Over 20 years of history, the United States development partnership with Russia had evolved to be very focused on specifically maintaining space for civil society organizations and supporting those organizations, primarily Russian-led organizations that sought to advance the principles of freedom of speech, freedom of civil society, openness, transparency, and government and public administration.

Obviously that specific space has been aggressively targeted with those organizations, whether they are USAID partners or otherwise, having been the subject of visits and raids and document requests and other things that have made it very hard for those organizations to continue their mission.

That said, our Ambassador in Russia and our State Department team in Russia is very focused on this element of the partnership and dialogue with that country. And, in fact, there are a range of mechanisms they can use to continue to provide support through international organizations and others to advance civil society causes. But at the end of the day, we are very concerned and worried about the continued restrictions on these organizations.

By the time what happened last year happened, USAID was a very small partner with these organizations that had become almost entirely supported through a diversity of sources of support, most of which were Russian. So it is not so much a targeting of USAID that we are concerned about. It is the space and the ability of partners, like GOLOS, to be effective operators.

Senator MURPHY. So without the mission presence, will there be any presence of USAID dollars in Russia moving forward?

Dr. SHAH. Well, the State Department will continue to provide engagement and support in a range of ways to partners. USAID will not be part of that.

Senator MURPHY. Just turning quickly to Afghanistan, I want to just raise a very specific point. On one of my recent visits there, we were taking a look at some, you know, very productive programs that you had funded to try to build the agricultural sector. And we continued to hear about a persistent problem of transport that, though we were doing a better job of getting resources to producers and they were producing new crops that were not poppy, increasingly they just could not come up with an economic rationale to get them out of the country to buyers because on average the transport was being stopped 24 different times, legally and illegally, by people who required them to pay fees. And by the time they got it to a port, it just did not make any sense to sell it any longer.

Can you talk a little bit about this specific problem in Afghanistan and how that potentially gets better or worse as we decrease our military presence there? We are doing a lot of good work with farmers, but it does not do much good if they cannot get their product to market because of the difficulty of transportation.

Dr. SHAH. Well, thank you for asking about agriculture in Afghanistan. I think over the next 5 to 7 years, until some of the mining resources come online, that will be the core driver of growth and development and employment for the bulk of the people of Afghanistan.

The reality is the central challenge for Afghanistan in this setting is sustaining the huge gains that have already been made, and ultimately replacing international support and military contracting with private activity and private investment. And private investment simply cannot thrive in an environment that, as you described, has so many erratic points of engagement from officials, or otherwise, who effectively create a difficult and sometimes corrupt operating environment.

So we have worked in a number of ways to address that. First we have created something called the Tokyo Mutual Accountability Framework by which future aid commitments will be conditioned on Afghans themselves achieving certain benchmarks, one of which is specifically fighting corruption and improving the collection of domestic revenue from customs and reducing transport bottlenecks.

Second, we work with them across the board on trying to, in a more specific way, implement programs that address these things. Things as technical as using mobile-phone-based payment systems have been found to be effective at essentially cutting out the various layers of middlemen who can sometimes cause these types of respective corruption problems that limit private activity and investment.

The third is we are in the process of making sustainable agricultural investments and often doing it through local Afghan private enterprises, and we think that is going to be a very important part of that sector succeeding.

Senator MURPHY. Thank you. Thank you very much, Mr. Chairman.

The CHAIRMAN. Senator Cardin.

Senator CARDIN. Thank you, Mr. Chairman.

Administrator Shah, I want to spend a little bit of time allowing you to respond to how the President's budget fits into the Rebalance to Asia policies that the administration has announced and is moving forward on so many different fronts. So I am interested as to how your budget will complement the President's initiative on the Rebalance to Asia. First, I want to ask about two specific countries, and then I will be glad to get a general response if the time remains.

In Burma, the President has made this a personal priority. You opened an office in August of last year, if I am correct. Can you just update us as to the progress being made in that country? We have gotten mixed reports as to how things are going.

Dr. SHAH. Yes, thank you. I will say just in general while we have a 6-percent overall reduction in our budget, the fiscal year 2014 request reflects a 7-percent increase for Asia to capture this Presidential priority of a pivot to a prioritization of our Asia partnerships.

In Burma specifically, when the President was there, he both opened the USAID mission and launched a partnership that was, in fact, conditional. It delineates the conditions under which we are expanding our efforts on a range of fronts. And some of those conditions have to do with government transparency and openness and continuing on their path of reform. And some of them have to do with how they are addressing the peace process with ethnic minorities in certain border areas.

We believe there has been effective and significant progress in the first area, and we know there are processes in place to address the second. But as we have all seen more recently in the press, that it is not on the same trajectory as the first.

That said, our efforts are focused on a few things. First, we are focused on improving the economic climate, opening up the economy, and supporting the kinds of public-private partnerships that we launched on a recent visit that I made there with a range of American technology companies creating higher education partnerships and opportunities for business starts in Burma.

A second is a real focus on health, education, and agriculture, which are by indicators some of the lowest in the region by far on all of those fronts, and they have a lot of potential. But we will have to implement those programs effectively and with far more domestic investment alongside our commitments and capabilities.

And then the third is we are active participants in the peace process and in the humanitarian services needs that exist in areas where there has been ethnic conflict. And so we are actively doing that as well.

Senator CARDIN. I would suggest there is no bigger spotlight than the President when he visits, but you need to keep the spotlight on Burma. Clearly the progress has been inconsistent and there is great opportunity there.

I want you to comment on Vietnam for one moment, and let me put this in context. It is one of the PEPFAR countries, and I am a strong supporter of PEPFAR. I think it has been incredibly successful. But in Vietnam, PEPFAR makes up more than half the aid programs we have there, totaling roughly $70 million dollars if I am correct. And that is a significant amount of money for that one country.

I believe that the HIV/AIDS rate in Vietnam is less than .05 percent. So the question is, Is that the best use of our foreign aid resources in a country that has a relatively low rate of infection, where the other needs are so great? That money, perhaps, could be used for other purposes to advance U.S. goals. Your comments.

Dr. SHAH. Well first, thank you for asking the question. I think the President's budget, especially in fiscal year 2014, reflects some of those tough tradeoffs. While we remain very committed to the PEPFAR control effort in Vietnam, the actual budget committed to that will decrease significantly by 20 percent, because of increased domestic investment and responsibility for seeing through the on-going treatment needs for Vietnamese patients, but also because we wanted to increase resources in a few other areas of investment in order to capture opportunities on poverty reduction, and maintain civil society rights, and support democratic governance.

Senator CARDIN. You are usually very responsive to my questions. I did not find that particularly responsive. We have a limited amount of money, and it is wonderful their country is making progress on HIV/AIDS, but, are there higher priorities that we should be investing in in Vietnam?

Dr. SHAH. Well, let me address it a slightly different way by saying I think one of the top priorities we do want to capture is Vietnamese participation in the TPP, the trade partnership. And we are increasing our investment to encourage that participation, and the budget reflects that in that it reflects an increase in our economic support resources, but a decrease in some of the core global health investments.

There are other programs we are seeing through, like dioxin remediation and support for overall economic governance. But I think the direct answer to your question is, yes, we believe that there are other priorities that we should be supporting, and we are trying to prioritize that within a difficult budget.

Senator CARDIN. And there is strong support for PEPFAR, and I think it has been remarkably successful. My point is that if there are higher leverage programs available in a country, we should be able to talk about that and look at it. Vietnam has been in the spotlight a lot for United States relations, and it is a country that we have made a lot of progress with, including on security issues. I think many of us thought that is amazing.

So we have made progress on all fronts of Vietnam, and we have to look at our resources and see if we are using them most effectively.

I will get your response to the other parts of Asia later, but thank you very much for your commitment.

The CHAIRMAN. Senator Kaine.

Senator KAINE. Thank you again, Dr. Shah. I just want to follow up on comments that the chairman made about the Americas. Senator Rubio made some comments as well. And, you know, just to say that any time somebody from USAID or the State Department is here before this committee, I think you are going to hear a lot of questions about this from, I think, a lot of different angles because it is of grave concern.

I lived in Honduras in 1980 and 1981 when it was a military dictatorship. And in that period of time, labor activists, human rights activists, clergy were being persecuted, even losing their lives. There were civil wars in Guatemala and El Salvador that were sending refugees by the tens of thousands over the border. The United States was building a military presence in Honduras to use as a staging area for a fight against Nicaragua.

It is not a military dictatorship today. It is a democracy today, and it is less safe. The people that I lived with then in a very oppressive time are less safe in their communities today in Honduras, and not just in Honduras, than they were. At that point, Honduras, who has been just a spectacular ally of the United States—if there is a more pro-U.S. Government in Central America than Honduras, I do not know what it is over time.

We pulled the Peace Corps out of Honduras because it has the highest murder rate in the world. And so when we see budgets that are declining in this part of the world, it is not only—all the issues that the chairman mentioned are true. So many of the issues that we are wrestling with, they are right in our own front yard in the Americas. But we also have a little bit to do with this.

I met with the Honduran Ambassador to the United States yesterday. In terms of their internal security situation, you know, perceptible reductions in U.S. consumers' demand for drugs is the thing that would make them the safest. If we had a plant that was on the border of the United States that was spewing airborne toxins over Central America and killing people, we would do something about it. We would be demanded to do something about it. Our committees would demand that we do something about it.

But it is U.S. demand for drugs that is hugely a part of the security situation, especially in Central America. So whether it is CARSI, whether it is your rule of law, project to help Mexico and criminal justice issues, whether it is this Partnership for Growth pilot that you are working on in El Salvador, and that is something where there is a budgetary plus. I was glad to see that, El Salvador and other countries.

I just think before this committee and before the International Development Subcommittee, you know, I think you are going to hear a lot of questions about the Americas.

We may be rebalancing toward Asia because of China. China is rebalancing toward the Americas, as you know, with their work in resource contracts and so much of what they are doing in the Americas. You know, they see it as an opportunity area. They see it as an area where they should be more deeply involved.

I would venture to say, you know, it is probably hard to get transparent Chinese budgetary figures, but they have a development philosophy, too. And I would venture to say that their development philosophy, they see the Americas as a growth area for the Chinese development philosophy, and it is an area of decline for us. And I just think that it is something that we need to be very, very concerned about.

And I suspect that there will be an awful lot of questions about that any time State, USAID, other agencies are before this committee.

Dr. SHAH. Thank you. I appreciate those comments. I know they echo those of the chairman.

The CHAIRMAN. And the chair is happy to have an ally in this. [Laughter.]

Dr. SHAH. I will say in this context, we have worked very hard to have a dramatic investment in the CARSI Program to expand the Partnership for Growth to that region, and to enhance the public-private partnerships specifically for El Salvador, Guatemala, and Honduras, and even to establish this new program with the city of Los Angeles where we are not just taking the kind of technical strategies that have worked in that setting at crime reduction, but actually asking the specific individuals who worked to counter those specific gang organizations to go to Central America and work with counterparts that are facing, in some settings, the same gang organization.

You are absolutely right that there is a very close and compelling tie to what happens in this country and citizen security in that region. It is also very clear that the fundamental outcome of the Partnership for Growth is that the No. 1 constraint to growth is citizen security. That is far and away No. 1, and that is why we are trying to do everything we can against those challenges. And we have also expanded our efforts to do this in a coordinated way with the military and with the mapping exercises that SOUTHCOM has really taken leadership on.

We appreciate those comments, and I hear you, and I certainly hear the chairman as well.

The CHAIRMAN. Thank you. Let me just piggyback a moment so we can close the loop on this. I gave it to you in a long list of things, so I just want to mention specifically—on CARSI, how are you intending to use the additional funding for 2014? And in addition to what specifically are you using the additional funding for, what are we doing about helping or engaging the Central American governments in their fiscal and policy reforms that would be necessary to sustain these types of programs that were supported by AID?

Dr. SHAH. Well, thank you, Senator. I have had the chance to visit and see some of these efforts in practice, and our funding goes to specific elements of CARSI. CARSI obviously also includes core State investments. But some of the things we have supported include mapping, community crime—mapping using new technologies and identification of crime rates, areas, hot spots, community crime prevention strategies that have borne out with real data that they have been far more effective than what those communities were trying before.

We have been the lead partner within that program for some of the youth programs that reach at-risk youth and have engaged some American partners to help advance those efforts as well. And then we work in partnership to track both the international gang relationships and otherwise to be able to provide data and information to our partners in the region. Those are just some of the things that CARSI does overall, and we have one part of that program in terms of our responsibility.

On the very good question of what are we doing on the fiscal policy side, while I know there are some activities to support that, I would rather get the right answer for you and send that out.

The CHAIRMAN. I will look for that answer. So basically, is your answer that you are just plussing up the activities you are already pursuing under CARSI, or is there something new that you are doing with the additional money?

Dr. SHAH. No. Well, I think the things that we believe have the most evidence of being really effective are the areas where we will focus the increased resources. And this mapping effort that has offered a lot of data and information has been very closely correlated to improving outcomes is one of the examples of that.

The CHAIRMAN. Senator Murphy.

Senator MURPHY. Thank you, Mr. Chairman. One additional question. I wanted to bring you back to Russia's zone of influence again, talk about the Ukraine for a moment.

You know, obviously a pivotal moment right now in the Ukraine as they are making some fundamental decision as to which they orient. It is not a choice for them necessarily, but there is certainly a lot of leverage that we have at our disposal to try to make their turn to the West slightly more attractive than a turn to the east. The Peace Corps, for instance, has one of its largest presence in the world in the Ukraine. We have had enormous success there.

Can you just talk for a moment about the tools at our disposal at USAID over the next several years as we talk with Yanukovych and others about their opportunity to orient themselves toward Europe, to have greater partnership with the United States amidst obviously growing pressure Russia to look in a different direction.

What are the tools that we have at our disposal to try to help them make that decision?

Dr. SHAH. I think we have a few. We have helped to expand the Peace Corps presence as one example. We have supported democratic governance and civil society programming and have been probably the lead international supporter, and thereby have some very longstanding relationships and partnerships with organizations in that community. And many of them have matriculated into government and have taken with them a capacity to work with us and partner with us.

Traditionally, we have had a larger health investment in the Ukraine. Part of that was focused on the control of TB and helping them manage, in particular, multidrug resistant tuberculosis, which was more challenging. And more recently we are focused on establishing partnerships that can attract more private investment.

We do not have the kind of resourcing to allow for sort of large sale infrastructure, but we also do not think that is what is required given their economic standing. It is more helping them with policy reforms, domestic administration, and attracting private investment through our partners, including OPIC and Ex-Im and some of the other U.S. agencies that can bring resources to bear.

Senator MURPHY. Well, as you know, we are at a critical moment in terms of the decisions that are being made there, and I think you are right. At this point they are looking for opportunities for the United States to allow them to attract some private money that they right now do not have an availability to other than through partnerships with Russian industry. And I think you are along the right track.

Thank you, Mr. Chairman.

The CHAIRMAN. Thank you. Well, Mr. Administrator, thank you. You have exhibited a breadth and depth and scope of knowledge of your agency, and that is tremendously reassuring to the committee. We look forward to working with you on some of these issues that we think we can enhance. And as I visit abroad, I always like to stop by AID projects and see our men and women in action, and always impressed by them.

With the thanks of the committee, the record will be remain open until Friday.

The CHAIRMAN. And this hearing is adjourned.

[Whereupon, at 11:58 a.m., the hearing was adjourned.]

ADDITIONAL QUESTIONS AND ANSWERS SUBMITTED FOR THE RECORD

RESPONSES OF ADMINISTRATOR RAJIV SHAH TO QUESTIONS SUBMITTED BY SENATOR ROBERT MENENDEZ

SYRIA

I understand that the United States has been the largest provider of humanitarian aid to Syria and I commend the administration on all it has done on this front. But given the scale and scope of the crisis and the exponential growth in the number of refugees, I believe we should be doing more and we should also be ensuring that we receive credit for the contributions we are making.

Question. Do you expect a dramatic increase in the level of support for Syrian humanitarian assistance over the next few months?

Answer. For the past 2 years, the U.S. Government has continuously programmed humanitarian funds in Syria and the neighboring countries to respond to evolving needs on the ground, targeting any available opportunities to get assistance to people in need. Given the protracted conflict and continuously growing needs, the Syria response will remain one of the USG's highest humanitarian priorities. USAID anticipates that emergency food requirements in Syria and neighboring countries will double by October, requiring a commensurate increase in support from the USG and other donors. For example, the U.N. World Food Programme (WFP) is currently reaching approximately 2 million people in Syria with emergency food assistance, with plans to expand distributions to 4 million people. USAID and the U.S. Department of State's Bureau of Population, Refugees, and Migration (State/PRM) are in the process of programming additional funds, which will be announced be in the coming months.

Question. How can we ensure that we receive credit for all the contributions we are making? How do we balance the need to receive credit from the Syrian people, with the imperative of protecting aid providers by not labeling everything as ''made in the USA?''

Answer. Though recognition of U.S. humanitarian efforts inside Syria are severely constrained by safety and security concerns we are working to make our aid more visible. The U.S. Government requires NGO partners to brand our assistance unless doing so would imperil the lives of aid recipients and the humanitarian workers delivering assistance. In the majority of Syria it remains too dangerous for wide-scale branding activities. In areas where it is safe to do so, including opposition held areas in the north, we are able to inform local leaders and recipients about where the aid is coming from.

We work with international organization partners to highlight U.S. Government support wherever possible. For example, nearly all of the bakeries receiving U.S. Government flour in Aleppo governorate are informed that it is U.S.-donated flour. A USG partner recently delivered heavy-duty plastic sheeting branded with the USAID logo to Atmeh camp in Idlib governorate. The plastic sheeting will be used to construct community structures in the camp, which houses more than 26,500 IDPs. The USG continues to work with partners to evaluate appropriate opportunities to increase the visibility of USG assistance without endangering the lives of both partners and beneficiaries.

Because wide-scale branding is not an option at this time, we are seeking to get the word out in other ways that do not undermine the operation: U.S. Government staff in D.C. regularly meet with the Syrian diaspora community to utilize its connections inside Syria and spread the message of USG support. We also continue to heavily engage with local, regional, and international media, both traditional and digital, to illustrate the extent to which USG humanitarian assistance is reaching a wide range of areas inside Syria.

U.S. Government officials use every public opportunity to highlight our humanitarian assistance to the region, including speaking engagements, social media, and regional, national, and international media interviews.

Question. Should we be providing more of the humanitarian aid through the Syrian opposition as some have suggested? Or are you satisfied with the current approach of going primarily through the United Nations?

Answer. As policy, the USG does not channel humanitarian assistance through political organizations and institutions, such as the Syrian Coalition or the Syrian Arab Republic Government (SARG). To reach all populations in need, the USG and all other humanitarian donors must work with relief organizations that strictly adhere to the humanitarian principles of neutrality and impartiality of aid. This is particularly essential in a war zone, to ensure access to beneficiaries as well as the safety of beneficiaries and the relief workers who are delivering the aid.

The USG continues to closely work with the Syrian Coalitions' Assistance Coordination Unit (ACU) on humanitarian activities and is currently funding a humanitarian advisor for 3 months to improve the ACU's capacity to better coordinate and manage the humanitarian response in Syria.

While the USG is delivering approximately 56 percent of its assistance in Syria through U.N. agencies, the USG also provides a significant portion of funding to international NGOs that are delivering assistance through networks of local NGOs. The USG's strategy is based on the ability of relief organizations, whether U.N. agency or NGO, to respond to needs quickly and effectively.

To date, USG humanitarian assistance has reached all 14 governorates, including contested and opposition-controlled areas. The World Food Programme (WFP), which receives significant support from the USG, is working in coordination with the Syrian Arab Red Crescent and its vast network of volunteers, as well as NGOs, to reach nearly 2 million people during each distribution cycle. In addition, USG support through international NGOs has reached more than 1 million people in some of the hardest hit areas of Syria. The USG will continue its funding strategy, while also working to identify potential new partners that can reach underassisted areas or respond to unmet needs.

LATIN AMERICA GENERAL

Our international affairs budget should more accurately reflect the importance of relationships, opportunities, and challenges in our own hemisphere. Latin American and Caribbean nations are our neighbors, and our actions in the hemisphere have a direct, often magnified, impact at home.

Question. What are USAID's objectives for foreign assistance in the region? How will reductions in funding affect USAID's ability to achieve those objectives?

Answer. Impressive progress in the Latin America and Caribbean (LAC) region in the past several decades has enabled USAID to adjust its mission in the region away from providing direct assistance—like vaccinations and food aid—and toward strengthening the capacity of LAC governments, the private sector and civil society to propel their own development.

We are prioritizing investments in four areas: (1) rebuilding Haiti through investments in agriculture, infrastructure, energy, health and economic growth; (2) reducing crime and violence—particularly among youth in Mexico, Central America, and the Caribbean—and reducing drug production in Colombia and Peru; (3) promoting democracy and protecting fundamental freedoms in Cuba and other countries where restrictions on press and civil society and flawed electoral processes continue, and in some cases worsen; and (4) reducing greenhouse gas emissions and adapting to the impacts of global climate change.

To accelerate progress in these areas, we are embracing a new way of doing business by: (1) channeling more resources through local entities; (2) testing novel ways to help local governments generate revenues for development; (3) partnering with private companies (U.S., multinational, and local) to supplement our assistance, create durable local enterprises and deliver long-term development dividends; (4) opening USAID to innovators from LAC and the world in search of the most effective and efficient development solutions; and (5) tapping into the home-grown development expertise of LAC leaders like Brazil, Chile, Colombia, and Mexico.

CUBA

I have long-supported a strong budget allocation for U.S. democracy promotion funding in Cuba. Our efforts on this score provide critical support to Cuba's civil society such as access to communication technology, humanitarian assistance for the families of political prisoners, and training for independent journalists. It is essential that we uphold the historical funding level of $20 million to demonstrate our strong support in Cuba for democracy, freedom of expression and assembly, and human rights. This year's request is only $15 million.

Question. What are the reasons for these cuts?

Answer. The U.S. commitment to human rights and democracy in Cuba remains strong. We will continue our robust program providing humanitarian support to political prisoners and their families, building civil society and expanding democratic space, and facilitating the information flow in, out, and within the island.

The FY14 request for $15M is based on our assessment of needs on the ground, and on-island and off-island capacity to carry out programs. In addition, the combined pipeline (FY09 to FY12) for Department of State and USAID implementers is about $44 million, sufficient funding ($74 million total) to carry out the purposes of the program over the next 3 years.

MEXICO

I understand that the nature of our assistance delivery to Mexico has changed. Whereas in the early stages of the Merida Initiative, we delivered a good deal of expensive equipment, we are now working to support the Mexican Government's efforts to strengthen institutions. However, I want to make certain that—as we reduce our assistance budget to Mexico by almost 40 percent—we are not constraining our ability to flexibly respond to any strategy shifts that may come down under the new Mexican administration.

Question. Do we have the flexibility to respond to policy shifts that may emerge under President Peña Nieto? USAID is also supporting municipal level crime prevention programs in Mexico for the first time. What lessons can be learned from similar efforts that have been going on in Central America for several years?

Answer. Yes, USAID has the flexibility to respond to potential policy shifts from the new Peña Nieto administration. In fact, the Peña Nieto administration expressed support for USAID's primary areas of Merida Initiative programming—criminal justice reform, crime and violence prevention, and human rights. Closely aligned with the priorities of the new administration, USAID continues to emphasize crime prevention and community resiliency under Pillar IV of the Merida Initiative. While the geographic and technical focus may change as the Government of Mexico (GOM) develops its new approach to crime prevention, USAID and our counterparts are currently working together to align strategic priorities and activities.

USAID has incorporated lessons learned from crime prevention programs in Central America to its programming in Mexico, where USAID supports the GOM and local communities to plan and implement community development strategies aimed at reducing crime and violence and providing youth with alternatives to crime. The Pillar IV strategy and current programs relied heavily on lessons learned from Central America, in particular the need to improve coordination and planning at the local level through the development of municipal crime prevention committees and plans. USAID is also incorporating experience in crime data collection and analyses, as well as in establishing alliances with the private sector to reduce crime and violence.

COLOMBIA

Colombia is working toward implementation of some ambitious but necessary reforms and I am glad that USAID is supporting them in these efforts. The Land Restitution and Victims Law, in particular, is essential for sustainable peace in Colombia. Colombia is taking on a greater share of the counternarcotics burden. I am happy to see that. I understand, also, that Colombia is increasingly involved in training and assistance delivery elsewhere in Latin America. Years of U.S. training has prepared Colombian security officials for the task of assisting their neighbors—a sound U.S. investment. Colombia and the FARC are in the middle of a peace process right now. We all long to see lasting peace in Colombia and are hopeful for an accord.

Question. Will this budget request allow us to respond if the Colombians call on us for assistance? For help implementing a peace accord?

Answer. USAID is supporting many Government of Colombia (GOC) efforts that lay the groundwork for peace. Our current programs are focused on bringing state presence and services to marginalized, high-conflict areas of the country; supporting victims and land restitution; and promoting access to justice. Many of these programs directly support GOC initiatives related to the five agenda items (rural development, guarantee of functional political opposition and civic participation, end of conflict, drug trafficking, and rights of victims) to be negotiated by the FARC and Colombian Government as part of a possible peace accord.

Without knowing what the GOC may or may not request in terms of additional or modified support in light of a possible peace agreement, we have worked to increase flexibility in our programs in order to quickly adjust our assistance if need be.

CENTRAL AMERICA

CARSI is a top priority. I am glad to see the President's request includes an addition $27 million for security in Central America. However, I believe our efforts in this region could benefit from more robust assistance levels. Central American nations face grave challenges—Honduras' homicide rate is among the highest in the world. The U.S. Government is partnering with governments in Central America to prevent violence, strengthen state institutions, combat narcotics trafficking, and increase citizen security. Failure to adequately fund these efforts will result in continued high levels of crime and violence, and an inability to dismantle criminal organizations. U.S. investments in the region expand markets for American businesses and connect high quality Latin American goods to the U.S. market. Stable Central American countries diminish the push factors for illegal immigration.

Question. To what extent are the governments of Central America implementing fiscal and policy reforms necessary to sustain and replicate programs currently supported by USAID? How does USAID intend to use the additional CARSI funding requested for FY 2014? Is the additional funding sufficient to meet the challenges we face in Central America?

Answer. Central American nations are making progress toward raising more of their own resources to improve the rule of law and address the root causes of crime and insecurity in their countries.

For example, El Salvador has improved its tax collection system, which should generate additional funding for citizen safety initiatives. Similarly, Honduras passed an emergency "security tax" measure in June 2012 that established a temporary levy on a range of financial transactions with the proceeds set to support security sector needs.

In addition to continuing to implement programs for at-risk youth, municipal crime prevention, and rule of law, USAID intends to use additional FY14 CARSI funding to further target the most vulnerable, at-risk populations.

For example, USAID is partnering with the city of Los Angeles to adapt a tool designed to identify those youth most at risk of joining a gang. Using this tool, USAID will provide mentoring and family support services on those most vulnerable to joining gangs and criminal activity.

Further, USAID will continue to pursue public-private partnerships on social prevention to engage local actors and maximize private sector contributions. For example, USAID recently signed a partnership with five Salvadorian foundations to combat citizen insecurity and strengthen municipal responses to crime and violence in 50 dangerous communities in El Salvador.

Finally, USAID works actively to incorporate best practices and lessons learned in other parts of the region and world into our citizen security portfolio. FY14 funding will help USAID develop and nurture best practices among citizen security technical experts and practitioners from various cities across the Western Hemisphere.

CARSI assistance is meant to supplement—not supplant—the need for host nations to develop, fund, and implement national strategies to reverse their deteriorating citizen safety environments.

USAID has effectively coordinated our programming with other donors and multilateral and international financial institutions to reduce duplicative programs and identify leveraging opportunities to enhance the impact of our funding. Together with other donors and the host country governments, the nearly $132 million appropriated for USAID-specific CARSI programs in Central America from FY08 through FY12 has been able to achieve results in targeted municipalities and provide the host countries with blueprints for successful interventions to address the underlying drivers of crime and violence.

CARIBBEAN

The Caribbean is a transshipment point for drugs en route to the United States. The Caribbean Basin Security Initiative aims to improve local capacity to combat the flow of illicit drugs. However, I worry that we are not doing enough. The sequester is reducing our military's presence in the Caribbean, certain interagency interdiction programs were grounded for off the coast of Central America for other reasons, and this budget request, instead of compensating for these losses, decreases funding for Caribbean security.

Question. Are our development and crime prevention activities in the hemisphere well-coordinated, strategic, and forward-looking?

Answer. Since 2010, various USG agencies, including USAID and the State Department, have been jointly implementing Caribbean Basin Security Initiative (CBSI) programs to reduce illicit trafficking, increase citizen security and address the causes of crime and violence. In an interagency effort, we have drawn on each other's comparative advantage to provide assistance on maritime and aerial security cooperation, law enforcement capacity building, border and port security and firearms interdiction, justice sector reform, and crime prevention and at-risk youth. In addition, the Department of State convenes an Inter-Agency Working Group including representatives from USAID, DHS, DOJ, ATF, DEA, OSD, SOUTHCOM, NORTHCOM, and USCG to discuss CBSI programs and related strategies.

USAID has taken a strategic and coordinated approach to addressing the security and development needs in Latin America and the Caribbean. The CBSI programs complement the Central America Regional Security Initiative (CARSI) and the Merida Initiative in Mexico. As trafficking activities are being prevented in one area, traffickers seek alternative routes, so there is a need to preemptively deter trafficking activities from taking root in other areas. One mechanism to help ensure that these initiatives are effectively coordinated is the Executive Committee for citizen security in the Western Hemisphere. This interagency group includes key interagency stakeholders in each of the initiatives and brings them together periodically to discuss lessons learned, opportunities for enhanced implementation, and opportunities for coordination across the initiatives.

USAID missions in El Salvador, Guatemala, Honduras, Jamaica, the Dominican Republic, and Barbados and the Eastern Caribbean are developing strategies that include citizen security as a key focal point for the planning of long-term development activities. The idea of cross-sectoral responses to the security environment is woven throughout and integrated into these programs with the goal of improving citizen security. For example, at-risk youth who participate in USAID's workforce development programs benefit from life skills and vocational training that are interconnected with broader health programs. All of these activities work in concert to ensure that youth who are at risk of engaging in criminal activities are receiving critical services and have opportunities to engage productively in society.

AFGHANISTAN/PAKISTAN

Question. I took my first trip as chairman to Afghanistan and Pakistan because I believe this region remains critical to our national security interests. The region is in the midst of an economic, security, and political transition. During my trip there, I spent time with our USAID missions and conducted field visits to review some of our aid programs. I came away impressed with the dedication and drive of our USAID teams there. But I also had concerns about how well we can conduct oversight in the field, given the security conditions.

♦ How are we right-sizing our aid presence in both countries to reflect our dimin- ishing footprint, security concerns, and implementation challenges we face? What steps are we taking to ensure that our aid is ''necessary, achievable, and sustainable,'' steps this committee called for in its June 2011 oversight report?

Our relationship with Pakistan has been rocky these past couple of years, despite efforts to build a strategic partnership based on mutual interests and trust. Efforts such as the historic Kerry-Lugar-Berman aid legislation have faced an array of political and implementation problems.

♦ What is your vision for improving this relationship, and how can Congress best support this effort given all the challenges we face?

Answer. *Afghanistan:* USAID has identified three priority areas for continued investment leading up to and beyond transition: sustainable, inclusive economic growth; credible, effective, and legitimate governance; and consolidation of gains, particularly in health, education, and women's rights. All programming will reflect the four principles of Results, Partnership, Sustainability, and Accountability, and USAID has adjusted its operating model to facilitate an Afghan-led and hence, more sustainable transition:

• First, USAID has increased the percentage of our programming provided on-budget to the Afghan Government, with an emphasis on building Afghan capacity to effectively manage and oversee this assistance. We will also continue to employ multilateral funds like the Afghanistan Reconstruction Trust Fund to consolidate programming and share monitoring responsibilities with other donors and the Afghan Government.
• Second, USAID is focusing more of its assistance on Regional Economic Zones (REZs) that cover major population centers and are linked with regional trade routes to generate more investment opportunities.
• Third, USAID is expanding the number and type of tools in our monitoring capacity to ensure we have access to all appropriate techniques necessary to provide continued oversight of our projects in the field, even as we decrease field staff and have potentially less direct hire access to project sites. This remote monitoring program will employ a number of methods in a multilayered approach to obtaining necessary information, including expanded partner reporting, remote sensing with aerial and satellite imagery where applicable, third-party monitors, community-based reporting, and collection/sharing of data gathered by other donors.
• Finally, in keeping with the principles of Busan, the New Deal for Fragile States, and the Tokyo Mutual Accountability Framework, USAID is transforming its investment approach in Afghanistan to one of mutual accountability, working in close partnership with the Afghan Government and its people and closely monitoring progress on reform. In July, we announced the creation of an incentive mechanism that will provide up to $175 million of current funding for the achievement of specific economic and democratic reforms before those funds are made available to the Afghan Government.

In addition to adjustments in USAID's operating model in preparation for transition, USAID has incorporated sustainability analysis into its project design process as part of the Administrator's Sustainability Guidance issued in 2011. Each project must develop a thorough sustainability plan during the design phase. To ensure that current and planned projects are consistent with the Sustainability Guidance, USAID also conducts internal portfolio reviews twice a year and once a year with the Afghan Government.

Answer. *Pakistan:* USAID agrees that programs in Pakistan must have the ownership of the Pakistanis to be fully successful and sustainable. USAID constantly monitors and evaluates our activities in Pakistan to ensure resources are used strategically and appropriately to achieve program goals and sustainability.

In 2011, USAID and the State Department jointly reviewed the program portfolio, streamlined the number of programs, and narrowed the focus to five priority sectors that represent mutual U.S. Government and Government of Pakistan priorities: energy, economic growth and agriculture, stabilization, education, and health. This more-focused portfolio of activities ensures that our investment:

- Advances U.S. foreign policy objectives;
- Defines ambitious, measurable, and achievable results and manages to these results;
- Builds local capacity in Pakistani governmental and nongovernmental organizations;
- Creates a network of public-private partnerships that makes gain sustainable;
- Safeguards U.S. Government resources; and,
- Communicates impact to a broad Pakistani audience to ensure visibility and awareness of our efforts.

USAID takes a multilayered approach to monitoring and evaluation in Pakistan, to include a missionwide third party contract for evaluations to ensure robust program management. Also, the number of locally employed staff has increased over the past year, although challenges continue. For example, earlier this year, USAID made the decision to relocate local staff operating out of our Peshawar office to Islamabad in response to the deteriorating security situation in Peshawar. Nevertheless, we believe we are able to continue effective monitoring of our projects in FATA using third parties, aerial and satellite imagery, and other methods.

USAID REFORM

USAID Reform USAID went through a period of 20 years of decline in personnel, dispersion of development responsibilities to other agencies such as the Millennium Challenge Corporation (MCC) and the State Department AIDS Coordinator's office, and in 2006, a loss of budgeting and policy capabilities.

Question. How would you assess your agency's progress in restoring its capacities under USAID Forward and the Development Leadership Initiative? What further reforms are you planning on making? What is the end goal of these efforts?

Answer. *USAID Forward:* USAID Forward, initiated in 2009, is designed to change the way the Agency does business—with new partnerships, an emphasis on innovation, and a clear focus on results.

The USAID Forward reform agenda identifies seven areas of concentration. They are: (1) implementation and procurement reform; (2) talent management; (3) rebuilding policy capacity; (4) strengthening monitoring and evaluation; (5) rebuilding budget management; (6) science and technology; and (7) innovation.

With these areas of priorities foremost, USAID established the Bureau of Policy, Planning and Learning to drive policy, and to restore and deepen the discipline of development across the Agency. Concurrently, USAID reestablished Agency-level budget and resource planning capability with the creation of the Office of Budget and Resource Management (BRM). USAID is responsible for the development and humanitarian assistance budget for USAID-managed programs, which is annually reviewed by the State Department and OMB. BRM has been instrumental in USAID's efforts to focus and concentrate development and humanitarian assistance in a difficult budget environment and strengthen budget capacity within all levels of USAID.

A cornerstone of USAID Forward has been the reestablishment of USAID strategic planning, including 5-year, country/regional based strategic plans, and project design capabilities. Under USAID Forward, the Agency established seven policies (ranging from education to gender equality to resilience) to support an evidence-based reform process and tighten and align Agency planning, budgeting, and reporting around the globe.

To date, USAID has conducted 21 design and 18 strategic planning workshops in the field. USAID missions are carrying out intensive and data-driven strategic planning. By the end of 2012, 20 USAID missions have approved strategic plans, Country Regional Development Cooperation Strategies. A total of 70 USAID missions are scheduled to complete their strategic plans by the end of the 2014. To better measure the effectiveness of programs and help to inform the next phase of programming, USAID field missions completed 186 quality program evaluations. These are driving USAID's evidence-based decisions.

The Agency has built several global platforms to capture results and leverage this knowledge so that it is shared transparently to further support and catalyze Agencywide learning capacities. Last, USAID has put in place structures to foster innovative development solutions (e.g., Grand Challenges, competitions, university partnerships) that create opportunities to connect staff to leading innovators in the private sector and academia. This will fortify new, effective partnerships across the globe to transform our collective efforts and help solve the most difficult development issues of today.

Taken together, these reforms are forming the foundation of a new model for development and will continue to define the way we work. It is a model that recognizes that the problems we face are solvable, but that solving them requires continued commitment and partnerships across the private sector, with NGOs, governants, universities, and others. Our ultimate goal remains to work ourselves out of business and replace our efforts with those of responsible institutions, vibrant private sectors, and thriving civil societies.

The Development Leadership Initiative: The Development Leadership Initiative (DLI) program was launched to increase USAID's total Foreign Service staffing by 1,200 with particular emphasis on rebuilding the technical cadre of agriculture, education, engineers, and economists, and expanding language capabilities and USAID's overseas presence. USAID's on-board Foreign Service Officer (FSO) career staff at the beginning of FY08 was 1,029, with about 640 of these deployed overseas. Cumulatively, with DLI funding from FY08 to FY10, USAID hired 720 new FSOs over attrition, averaging one new group of FSOs approximately every 8 weeks. FY11 funding supported an additional 100 new FSOs, bringing the total DLI hiring to 820 since its inception. No funds were appropriated for additional increases in FSO staff in FY12.

Recruitment and Hiring: DLI hiring is designed to rebuild USAID's technical capabilities as well as provide resources to enhance the Agency's stewardship functions. USAID has had a broad and rich applicant pool since its inception. Between 2008 and 2011, USAID received over 35,000 applications. The selection process is rigorous and highly competitive and approximately 15 percent of basically qualified applicants are invited for the three-stage interview process. Approximately 4 percent of applicants receive offers. While not required for all positions, most require a master's degree as a minimum qualification. On average, selected applicants have 5 to 7 years of prior international experience before joining USAID; most speak at least one other language; and about 28 percent are former Peace Corps Volunteers or staff.

Individuals hired through the DLI program now constitute 45 percent of the USAID Foreign Service. With a current cadre of 1,790 career FSOs, USAID has now reached almost 70 percent of its original hiring target.

Continued reform efforts are planned to build the capacity among the staff hired under the DLI program. These officers will need to have a strong foundation in core technical competencies relevant to their functions in the Agency to implement effective projects and to elevate development as an evidence-based discipline. Efforts are also underway to strengthen the alignment of staff globally with mission needs to advance USAID Forward reforms.

GLOBAL HEALTH PROGRAMS

U.S. global health programs are literally saving millions of lives. Over 5 million people with HIV are on treatment. We are well on the way to cutting malaria deaths in half in Africa by 2015. And USAID is rightly focused on preventing the preventable, namely helping countries save many of the nearly 7 million children under 5 who die every year, over 40 percent within that first vulnerable month of life. But, as effective as these programs are, efforts like the Global Health Initiative have struggled with interagency differences and tensions.

Question. Please explain to us the current status of the Global Health Initiative. How can USAID, CDC, and PEPFAR most effectively work together while each brings their comparative advantage to bear on some of the world's most pressing problems?

Answer. Leadership of USAID, CDC, and the Office of the Global AIDS Coordinator continue to meet on a regular basis to discuss policy issues related to our collective work in the field. In addition, there are technical committees that address cross-cutting issues, such as monitoring and evaluation, which are structured around the comparative advantages of the three agencies to produce the greatest results. Over 40 USG-supported countries have written strategies for operationalizing the Global Health Initiative and in-country teams work together to achieve the goals outlined in these strategies.

FOOD AID REFORM AND FOOD SECURITY

The administration has proposed some dramatic changes to the way we provide emergency food assistance.

Question. While there are many reforms proposed for food aid, the budget still continues to draw a pretty bright line between emergency assistance and programs to relieve chronic food insecurity. Is this something of a false dichotomy? Could we do more to promote resilience while helping address emergencies?

Answer. Emergency food assistance is provided first and foremost to save lives. Emergency resources can play a significant role in laying the foundation for greater resilience. The flexibility provided by having a range of tools for emergency response (cash, vouchers, or in-kind) greatly increases our ability to reach people before their ability to recover has been eroded. If a household receives assistance before losing all productive assets (thereby losing any source of future income), it is much more likely to be able to recover and move forward.

Emergency assistance is rarely enough to ensure the future resilience of vulnerable households. By layering, sequencing, and integrating our programming to build resilience, relieve chronic food insecurity, and help vulnerable populations recover from recurrent shocks and stresses. USAID's Annual Program Statement amendment issued at the height of the Sahel food crisis last year reflects just that—by focusing on resilience building across the Sahel, giving priority to emergency food assistance applications that supported recovery activities targeting the most vulnerable populations.

The emergence of resilience as an organizing concept helps bridge the historical divide between humanitarian and development programming. Emergency assistance, including both relief and recovery programs, provides a foundation upon which resilience and development investments can build, particularly in places such as Northern Kenya where emergency and recovery assistance is required year after year. There, new resilience programs have been designed to anticipate and incorporate emergency resources as a proactive way of protecting social and economic gains in in the face of inevitable droughts and other shocks in the future. Over time, these programs aim to sustainably reduce humanitarian assistance needs—building community, local and national capacities to manage through drought without humanitarian crisis.

The goal of all USAID food assistance programming is to eventually eliminate the need for food assistance. USAID expects that its funds, whether emergency or development, will be used in complementary ways.

There is inherent complementarity between title II nonemergency programs—which aim to provide a "hand-up" to particularly vulnerable households and communities, and Feed the Future's (FTF) agriculture programs—which help countries and communities use agriculture to "move out" of poverty. Real progress is being made to fully leverage this complementarity. For example, in Bangladesh and Guatemala, new FTF projects are completely or partially colocated with title II nonemergency programs that are targeting the more vulnerable in the region with foundational support to improve their health and food security. In some cases, FTF is using the same international and local partners as Food for Peace (FFP). In these cases title II programs now can aim to "graduate" vulnerable but viable households who can benefit from value chain interventions being implemented by FTF. In several other countries, USAID has taken a "division of labor" approach, targeting agriculture development assistance resources in higher productivity areas, and title II development programs in more food insecure, disaster-prone areas (e.g., Haiti and Uganda). The aim in these countries is to ramp up agricultural productivity where potential is greatest, while building resilience and increasing economic opportunity in crisis-prone areas to lay the foundations for sustainable growth.

Question. Under your leadership, USAID has emphasized its identity as a learning organization. You have worked on the challenges of food security for a number of years. What have you learned from Feed the Future (FTF) and from your efforts to promote food aid reform? What has surprised you?

Answer. FTF and Food Aid Reform are both examples of the integrated and innovative approaches that USAID and the U.S. Government as a whole employ to address the complex challenges facing the world. Natural disasters are becoming more frequent, resulting in greater shocks and threats to food security worldwide.

USAID has seen firsthand how greater flexibility in food assistance programming can help us save lives in places where traditional food aid cannot go. Our FFP teams have put together smart, creative solutions to meet urgent needs in some of the toughest emergencies globally, and with greater flexibility, they can do even more.

This year, in particular, we have committed a large portion of our funding available for flexible use to respond to the crisis in Syria. That means we do not have the flexibility to reach tens of thousands of children in places like Somalia, Kenya, Pakistan, and the Democratic Republic of Congo.

FTF coordinates closely with FFP. In general, FFP food aid programs are community-based programs targeted to very poor or extremely poor households—"the poorest of the poor." Many of these households depend on agriculture for livelihoods—either from farming their own land or working on someone else's land. We have learned that many of these households are often unable to meet their family's basic food and nonfood needs for 12 months of the year. Constraints, such as limited land size and labor availability, reliance on less productive technologies and practices, and poor access to markets and inputs, make it very difficult for these communities and households to break out of poverty. FFP programs work at a local level, providing a safety net for these extremely vulnerable households and have a proven success record in many underserved communities around the world. Meanwhile, many FTF programs focus on value chains and aim to address constraints to agricultural productivity both within targeted geographic areas and, in terms of policy, at a national level. For example, if a lack of access to fertilizer and improved seed is a significant constraint to productivity, FTF engages the host government and other interested partners to identify key challenges and develop solutions.

As a result, FTF and FFP have learned to work in tandem to allow for an expanded focus on the resilience of vulnerable communities to the shocks that exacerbate food insecurity. For example, in order to combat the recent crises in the Horn of Africa and the Sahel, FTF programs include both longer term investments like increasing the commercial availability of climate-resilient crops and reducing trade and transport barriers, as well as Community Development Funds (CDF). CDF plays a catalytic role in bridging humanitarian and development assistance. CDF investments fund community-based interventions aimed at increasing the economic and nutritional resilience of the rural poor and accelerating their participation in economic growth. These programs bridge humanitarian and development objectives through expanded support for productive rural safety nets, livelihood diversification, microfinance and savings, and other programs that reduce vulnerability to short-term production, income, and market disruptions.

VIOLENT EXTREMISM

Question. In 2011, USAID came out with a policy regarding the development response to violent extremism and insurgency.

♦　　　　To what extent are you now able to measure the effectiveness of programming that targets drivers of violent extremism?

♦　　　　What are some successful examples of USAID's work in countering violent extremism and what have been some key lessons learned?

Answer. To support our monitoring and evaluation (M&E) learning for countering violent extremism (CVE), USAID commissioned a review of program monitoring and reporting systems that track progress in addressing violent extremism and insurgency (VE/I). The report, which reviewed M&E systems across a number of countries including Iraq, Kenya, the Sahel, Afghanistan, Pakistan, and Yemen, provided a series of recommendations for the Agency's VE/I Steering Committee as part of a larger endeavor to produce an operational guide and/or field handbook to assist USAID practitioners. The report concluded that indicators developed for USAID CVE programs have shown steady improvement and increasing sophistication over the period 2006 to 2012. Though measuring the effectiveness of programming in insecure environments is often costly and burdensome, USAID's experience and expertise in this area has improved dramatically. Our impact evaluation techniques now include randomized control trials, baseline surveys, household surveys, mobile technology, and focus group discussions among others. In global forums, USAID has been identified as an early leader in developing approaches for CVE program measurement.

Evidence shows that drivers of extremism are generally related to the enabling environment (e.g., poorly governed areas and weak security services), pull factors (i.e., social networks, group dynamics, and existence of radical institutions), and push factors (i.e., societal discrimination, economic exclusion, and frustrated expectations). USAID CVE programming is designed to mitigate those factors. Therefore, measuring the effectiveness of our programming often involves measuring the change in community perceptions vis-a-vis those drivers. In this way, programs are developing more systematic approaches to credibly document progress and impact, beyond just anecdotal evidence.

Typical CVE programming focuses on livelihoods, governance and civic participation, functioning state services, government legitimacy, security, youth engagement, attitudes of tolerance and moderation, among others. Each of those programs will have tailored indicators to measure if they reached the desired impact and, by proxy, mitigated the drivers to radicalization and violence.

Investments in M&E at USAID have increased significantly, and indicators of progress have shifted toward more complex, abstract, and meaningful concepts like youth empowerment, community outlook for the future, attitudes toward violence, and stabilization. Indicator sets are more likely to capture citizen experience, behavior, and perception as well as on-the-ground reality. There is a recognition that citizen perception can be volatile in uncertain, high-risk environments and that much-surveyed populations are likely to deliver set responses to frequently asked questions. Much more effort is being invested in trying to capture concepts that are difficult to measure and may have indirect causal links with preventing extremist recruitment, such as the provision of justice (believed to be a vital factor in stability and resiliency in Pakistan and Afghanistan). In these M&E efforts, USAID collaborates with other agencies, such as the Department of Defense, in sharing indicators and data.

USAID programs incorporate a mixed-methods approach to data collection, which allows M&E specialists to validate or cross-check the reliability of data from any given source and which also affords richer and more nuanced information for learning than reliance on any one quantitative or qualitative method.

In Pakistan, USAID's Karachi Youth Initiative and Youth in Southern Punjab programs were developed in 2012 to enable the U.S. Government to respond to the massive amounts of at-risk youth in areas vulnerable to recruitment by violent extremist groups. Covering specific geographic neighborhoods and regions, USAID's Office of Transition Initiatives in the Bureau for Democracy, Conflict, and Humanitarian Assistance is developing an innovative system to measure whether the desired outcomes of each activity are achieved. Utilizing its independent monitoring unit (IMU), USAID is surveying the participants of each activity using relevant portions of a standardized ''question bank.'' Comparing before and after responses, USAID aims to determine whether participants' perceptions, attitudes, and beliefs have changed during the course of the activity, as well as whether any intended developmental outcomes were achieved. By using a standardized set of questions, USAID will be able to determine which types of activities are more effective at yielding the desired outcomes. In addition, participants will be interviewed 6 and 12 months following project completion to determine whether there are any long lasting effects to activities there.

In Karachi and southern Punjab USAID has helped lead interagency efforts to pilot small activities at the community level in order to test out a variety of ways to target neighborhoods and communities. Some of these activities support vocational training, youth clubs, leadership conferences, sport tournaments, schools. All activities seek opportunities for ways to disseminate ideas of peace, tolerance, and positive relations within the community. In both Karachi and southern Punjab, the drivers of violent extremism are manifold and vary widely. In Karachi, the neighborhood of Lyari is plagued with gang violence whereas violence in the Sultanabad neighborhood adjacent to the U.S. consulate is driven primarily by religious extremism. There is no ''one size fits all'' approach that would be effective across the country so interventions must continually adapt to the changing local dynamics.

USAID's Kenya Transition Initiative in Eastleigh (KTI–E) was established in August 2011 to enable at-risk youth to reject extremism, which has become a growing threat to Kenya's stability. The Partner Performance Management Plan (PPMP) was developed to clarify expectations, ensure alignment with program goals and effectively use current program information. Indicators of the PPMP were selected based on KTI–E's overall strategic approach while assessing the main activities of the project. By assigning indicators at each level of the Results Framework, KTI–E is able to monitor whether the developmental hypothesis is being achieved. Each of KTI–E's activities is assessed and analyzed at multiple stages including at the concept phase, during implementation, and at activity closeout.

KTI–E has focused on supporting moderate views and nonviolence amongst youth. Areas of action have included sponsoring public debates on issues related to extremism, interfaith dialogue, training for youth in financial literacy and entrepreneurship, support for local government townhall style meetings, and support to the Ministry of Youth to bridge the gaps in services for Somali youth.

One set of activities supported ''Weekly Youth Debates'' implemented by the Nabad Doon (Peace Seeking) Youth Alliance. The grantee held weekly debates among Somali youth in which participants discussed issues related to extremism facing youth in Eastleigh. This created a constructive and peaceful environment for youth to express themselves on sensitive topics. Each debate had between 180 to 200 attendees and one debate was televised on the ''Somali'' television channel. Building on the success of the first two debate activities, KTI–E supported a grantee to expand an existing Web site to carry out an enhanced interactive platform engaging youth in positive online activities that reject extremism. Through these activities, KTI–E has found that participants involved with the youth debates have been highly engaged in their communities, particularly with advocating against violent extremism.

SUDAN

Question. Sudan today is at a crossroads, not so much in terms of its relationship with South Sudan but in terms of its own future. Its economy is in dire straits. It is waging war in South Kordofan, Blue Nile, and Darfur. And, as in many countries, its youth are increasingly willing to take to the streets to announce that the status quo is no longer acceptable. There are those who look at the operating environment in Sudan and argue that we should not have a full USAID mission until we can have full-scale development programs. I look at Sudan and think the opposite, as long as security assessments permit. We have massive humanitarian programs there that demand oversight. We want to find ways to help the Sudanese people have free and fair elections and hold their government accountable. We want to find ways to help bring peace to Sudan and promote good economic as well as political relations with Sudan.

♦ What is your vision for the USAID mission in Khartoum, including plans for staffing and how to pursue democracy and governance goals?

Answer. USAID is committed to a partnership with the Sudanese people and to ongoing development programming and humanitarian assistance for conflict-affected communities. We are working to increase the engagement and participation of citizens in Sudan's governance and vision for its future, and to prevent the escalation of local conflicts in flashpoint areas, strengthen the foundations for peace in Darfur, and enhance Sudan-South Sudan cross-border dialogue. USAID operates under multiple layers of executive and legislative restrictions that limit the extent of our engagement.

Since the period leading up to the historic January 2011 referendum on self-determination for southern Sudan and the subsequent independence of South Sudan, the international community, including the United States, has seen an increasingly restrictive and difficult operating environment in Sudan. The scope of USAID's programs has diminished since the Sudan mission reopened in 2006 to support implementation of the 2005 Comprehensive Peace Agreement (CPA).

Despite this challenge, USAID is supporting efforts among the Sudanese people to raise their voices in the public sphere and engage with the government in constructive ways. For example, USAID supports civic participation through consultations in Khartoum on the development and adoption of a permanent constitution, which was mandated by the CPA and committed to by President Bashir. Though the process has been slow and our assistance has been limited in scope, USAID has partnered with respected Sudanese partners, such as Ahfad University for Women, to conduct open discussions about constitutional issues.

Sudan is still plagued by internal conflict of varying severity throughout the country's peripheral areas, as well as simmering tensions between Sudan and South Sudan that have continued since the independence of South Sudan. In response, USAID is helping to strengthen Sudanese NGO and civil society capacity to address the causes and consequences of political conflict, violence, and instability. In addition, recognizing the importance of women and youth in Sudanese society, USAID consistently looks for ways to increase their capacity to engage in peace-building and strengthen civil society at local and national levels. For example, USAID has supported training for culturally influential women artists (called Hakamat) from Southern Kordofan and Darfur to become peace activists. A USAID grantee, the Human Security Initiative (MAMAN), has worked with these female artists to spread messages of peaceful coexistence and tolerance in their communities. In addition, USAID is committed to building the capacity of youth and civil society organizations nationwide to more effectively represent the interests and preferences of citizens. USAID is also supporting health clinics, schools, and water yards for livestock in the disputed Abyei Area to engage all communities in the area and to help reduce competition and potential conflict over scarce water sources.

Despite significant humanitarian needs in Sudan, humanitarian space has also been steadily shrinking further over time, with restrictions in Darfur broadened to other areas of Sudan, most recently in Blue Nile State and Southern Kordofan State. The recently issued Sudanese Directive on Humanitarian Assistance codifies restrictions on access and operations that USAID and its implementing partners have faced for many years. These policies and procedures severely constrain USAID's ability to fund and ensure effective implementation of assistance programs. Restrictions have been imposed on programs that the Government has itself repeatedly appealed to donors to support, such as for early recovery in Darfur. Despite these challenges, USAID continues to be the largest donor of humanitarian assistance in Sudan, providing support to those in need through health, nutrition, and water interventions. Where conditions of access and security permit, USAID strengthens local markets, livelihoods, and food security through early recovery initiatives. However, increased fighting throughout Darfur has undermined opportunities and prospects for sustained early recovery in many areas and USAID continues its focus on meeting emergency needs as a result of displacement and violence in Darfur.

Regarding staffing in Sudan, USAID has assigned the next Mission Director to Khartoum and is in the process of filling other staff vacancies with U.S. Foreign Service personnel. Unfortunately, as a result of a 180-day Ordered Departure (OD) from Sudan, which lasted the maximum limit of 6 months for ODs (from September 2012 until March 2013), a number of American Foreign Service officers based in Khartoum curtailed their assignments. We are working to recruit experienced U.S. staff to fill critical positions so that we can move forward with more effective program implementation and oversight. We also continue to implement a staffing plan to gradually restructure the Sudan mission as part of a larger, global effort to consolidate functions that USAID and State Department share. As part of this process, we continue to transfer responsibility for some administrative support and financial functions to the State Department and to other USAID missions in the region in alignment with the U.S. Government's consolidation process.

USAID looks forward to collaborating with Congress on charting the way forward for our assistance to Sudan.

TB

Question. Particularly given the rising levels of resistance and the global threat posed by multi and extensively drug resistant tuberculosis, please explain the proposed decrease in funding for bilateral tuberculosis programs and how that reduction would be carried out in terms of altered activities.

Answer. It is important to clarify that the U.S. Government (USG) commitment to reducing the burden of tuberculosis (TB) is unwavering. When taking into consideration the overall FY 2014 funding request for TB—made up primarily of funding from the U.S. Agency for International Development (USAID), and supported by the annual contribution to the Global Fund to Fight AIDS, Tuberculosis and Malaria (Global Fund)—we can continue to leverage and maximize those investments to achieve greater impact. The concern in the global health community appears to center on the structure of the FY 2014 Congressional Budget Request, which identified the USAID FY 2014 budget request that is a reduction over FY 2012 but did not fully capture additional investments made through the Global Fund. The Obama administration has demonstrated its strong support for the Global Fund with a request for $1.65 billion in FY 2014, maintaining the same level requested in FY 2013, which is a $350 million increase over FY 2012.

The USG's important role in TB is maintained within the aggregate request, as is our longstanding leadership role. The response to global health problems is a shared responsibility, and USAID is striving to maintain our leadership while strongly encouraging countries that have the ability to do more to increase their commitments.

It is also important to point out that we are on track to achieve the Millennium Development Goal (MDG) of halving TB mortality rates by 2015, and USAID is on track to meet the Global Health Initiative TB goals for reducing TB prevalence and diagnosing and initiating treatment for 57,000 new multi-drug-resistant TB (MDR–TB) cases. This outcome is a result of decades of collaboration between the USG, developing countries, and public and private partners. This achievement is notable and will be one of the only health-related MDGs met by 2015.

USAID is working diligently with developing countries to increase the amount of TB funding within their national health budgets. As examples, the Government of South Africa recently committed to increase domestic funding for TB and has committed to fully funding the national scale-up of GeneXpert by investing over $27 million on equipment and consumables. In addition, the Government of India has expressed willingness to increase TB funding by over 40 percent over the next 4 years to scale-up case detection and management of MDR–TB. The nature of our assistance is evolving, and as these countries increase their resources, USAID resources will direct technical assistance to scaling-up quality interventions and piloting innovative approaches, while building national and local capacity in partnership with the ministries of health.

USAID's leadership in TB has contributed to impressive gains—with worldwide mortality from TB falling 41 percent since 1990. In particular, USAID has been instrumental in making available key innovations, such as GeneXpert, as well as new drug regimens, and enhanced diagnosis and treatment. For example, USAID is funding clinical studies to develop shorter TB drug regimens, and if successful, would reduce the treatment of MDR–TB from 24 months to 9 months, thereby, improving treatment outcomes, and significantly lowering the cost of treatment. Additionally, USAID is introducing the newly approved drug Bedaquailine, supporting the development of a second-line drug market for MDR–TB, and investing in research for new drug development.

CLIMATE CHANGE

Question. I was pleased to see that USAID's Climate Change and Development Strategy includes as the third strategic objective, strengthening ''development outcomes by integrating climate change in USAID programming, learning, policy dialogues, and operations.'' This integration is important to the overall efficiency and success of the strategy.

◆ Therefore, please provide at least two examples how the Agency has been integrating the strategy within the following areas: programming, learning, policy dialogues, and operations.

Answer. One of the ways that climate change is being integrated into USAID programming is through the strategic planning process; all USAID missions are required to fully consider climate change as they develop their 5-year Country Development and Cooperation Strategies (CDCSs). USAID developed supplemental guidance that provides information to missions on requirements to integrate climate change programming into the CDCS planning process. Through this guidance and additional technical support, missions have been able to successfully integrate climate change into their CDCSs. The Southern Africa Regional CDCS, for instance, integrates climate change into policy and decisionmaking as a part of an objective to increase sustainable economic growth in targeted areas. As another example, the Bangladesh CDCS establishes improving responsiveness to climate change as interest to an overall goal of becoming a knowledge-based, healthy, food secure, and climate resilient middle-income democracy.

USAID is also working to develop results frameworks and targeted outcome indicators that measure climate change and development outcomes for work in sectors throughout the agency, drawing on expertise from many sectors including energy, water, food security, democracy and governance, and humanitarian assistance. By tracking these indicators, we will be able to learn more about the impacts that development efforts across the agency are having on climate change. In this vein, USAID is implementing 10 Integration Pilot Projects to examine innovations on how to integrate climate change mitigation and adaptation across Agency development priorities. We are now planning evaluations that will help us draw rigorous lessons learned from those experiences.

In December, USAID released policy and program guidance on ''Building Resilience to Recurrent Crisis.'' This policy recognizes that climate change is a critical factor contributing to the shocks and stresses that can produce recurrent crises and undermine development gains. Integration of climate change considerations in USAID's Resilience Policy is just one example of how USAID is integrating climate change into its policy dialogues.

Question. As the USAID Climate Change and Development Strategy notes, climate change impacts in the form of rising temperatures and increasingly variable rainfall (to name just a couple) are likely to undermine livelihoods and threaten food security in developing countries, including where USAID operates. At the same time, the U.S. Government has undertaken a significant global hunger and food security initiative known as ''Feed the Future.''

◆ Please provide three examples of how USAID has been integrating climate change into the Feed the Future program and how this integration promotes their mutual benefit.

Answer. Climate change is inextricably linked to food security because of its wide-reaching impact on agriculture and landscapes. The Feed the Future Initiative has integrated indicators related to natural resources management and climate resilience into its monitoring and evaluation system so that we can track the effectiveness of our programs. In addition, many of the USAID staff working on food security and climate change are colocated in the same field offices and work together to build sustainable economic growth. Programs are being designed in partnership in order to build stronger capacity among our partner countries to address these critical issues. Some specific examples of how climate change is being integrated into the Feed the Future program follow.

One key component of building climate change adaptation into food security and other development efforts is the development of vulnerability assessments, which assess expected climate impacts enabling necessary adjustments in development planning and implementation. The Uganda mission recently completed a comprehensive climate change vulnerability assessment for the agriculture sector. The assessment is generating insights for use in food security policy, programming, and investment decisions. The climate analysis showed average temperatures have already risen and that they will continue to rise. The analysis also points to changes in precipitation patterns and an increase in extreme weather events. Of the eight crops assessed, coffee, matooke, maize, and beans were determined to be the most vulnerable. The livelihood analysis found that 73 percent of households surveyed were highly vulnerable to climate change impacts. The most vulnerable households are at risk partly because they rely on crops like coffee, matooke, maize, and beans for income and food security, and partly because they lack the assets, financial capital, and nonagricultural sources of income that can help households endure times of stress. To ensure local decisionmakers are aware of the assessment, USAID's Uganda mission organized a week of meetings and workshops for more than 150 government, donor, research, and civil society stakeholders. A total of 50 stakeholders joined a 1-day Options Analysis Workshop where cross-sector teams identified specific adaptation options for the agriculture sector. Within the mission, the vulnerability assessment is already being used to design programs and interventions that increase adaptive capacity under the Uganda Feed the Future Value Chain Project. The assessment is also being used to ensure existing Feed the Future interventions are planning for potential climate change impacts.

Another way Feed the Future is supporting the development of resilient agricultural systems is by helping farmers cope with extreme weather events. For example, with the help of climate change adaption techniques taught by Feed the Future, a Cambodian fish farmer was able to save her pond when record seasonal floods hit in 2011. As the water levels started rising, aquaculture technicians from Feed the Future showed her how to install a tall netting fence to keep her fish from escaping the pond and to keep unwanted predators out. They also advised her on how to protect the fence so crabs and debris wouldn't cut holes in it. This farmer is now sharing the techniques she learned with her neighbors, who lost their ponds during the floods.

The Feed the Future Initiative is investing in multiple safeguards and adaptation strategies to prepare for and respond to a changing climate in Ethiopia. Ethiopia, one of the most food insecure countries in the world, sits in the cross-hairs of climate change patterns, and is endeavoring to cope with the multiple threats to food security, access to water, and even certain livelihoods. The productivity—and soon, even the basic viability—of its long-cycle crops is at risk. These crops, which provide up to 85 percent of the food grown in Ethiopia, have already seen 15-percent declines in rainfall, setting up a potentially dangerous and costly interaction between drought and declining agricultural capacity. Under the most likely climate change scenarios, cereal production in Ethiopia—and, indeed, much of east Africa—may drop 30 percent by 2030. During that period, food aid to the region would have to triple to make up for the shortfall.

For example, USAID is investing $5 million to carry out global-level research on making livestock more climate resilient in order to help people that raise livestock better adapt to climate change impacts. USAID will support research on the development, identification, and introduction of livestock that are disease resistant and heat tolerant, and capable of living on low quality forages and feeds without experiencing a decrease in meat and milk production.

Additionally, USAID's Ethiopia Mission's Capacity to Improve Agriculture and Food Security (CIAFS) program supports Ethiopia's efforts to transform its agricultural sector and improve food security for the Ethiopian people by providing targeted training on and raising awareness of best practices in agricultural development. The project strives to empower leaders to catalyze change, drive growth, and reduce poverty. During this reporting period CIAFS organized study tours for Ethiopians to learn innovative practices and technologies in agriculture and natural resource management, targeting technologies for adapting to climate change. CIAFS also promoted peer-to-peer learning on an organized a study tour to Mali and Niger pastoralist areas for Ethiopian pastoral stakeholders including representatives of pastoralist organizations, parliamentarians, and relevant ministry leadership and staff.

Question. I understand that as part of USAID Climate and Development Strategy, USAID is helping developing counties move toward low-carbon emission economic growth by promoting low emission development strategies (LEDS). As part of LEDS, please describe how USAID is working to increase access to renewable and sustainable energy.

◆ Please provide examples of this work in Africa and Asia. In addition, in cases where energy is considered a constraint to growth, please describe how is USAID working to promote access to renewable and sustainable energy?

Answer. A LEDS is a planning and implementation framework that helps a country achieve its economic and social development objectives while reducing greenhouse gas emissions and building greater climate resiliency. USAID'S Enhancing Capacity for LEDS (EC–LEDS) program integrates economywide analysis and climate change mitigation considerations into long-term country-level planning and decisionmaking and assists countries to implement the clean and renewable programs that are identified as part of these strategies.

In Africa, USAID's LEDS work is just getting started. Negotiations on government-to-government Memorandum of Understandings (MOUs) have established jointly agreed work programs under EC–LEDS with Gabon, Zambia, Malawi, Kenya, and South Africa. As these work programs are being negotiated, our teams in-country have been working to put in place the necessary technical assistance mechanisms to provide targeted assistance to our partner countries in Africa that responds to the needs and actions outlined in the work programs. Examples of our clean energy-related work through EC–ELDS in Africa follow.

In Gabon, we are working with the Department of Energy's National Laboratories to build capacity for carbon footprint analysis of economic development and infrastructure projects, for public sector energy efficiency, and for cross-sectoral modeling. These efforts will enhance capacity for carbon footprint analysis of economic development and infrastructure and improve investment decisions that provide economic, social, and environmental value, backed by business cases that are sustainable, transparent, and accountable to society. This work will also build capacity to assess energy efficiency opportunities in the public sector and pilot demonstration projects with the goal of transferring analysis and implementation capabilities to the Ministry of Energy.

In South Africa, the principal objective of the EC–LEDS partnership is to strengthen public sector-related development planning and project development capacity for low emission projects, including the mobilization of development finance and private sector participation in such projects. This collaboration will provide support for the preparation and development of approximately 20–30 identified projects over the initial 3-year period. This will enable low emission projects to leverage potential development financing, cofunding and private sector participation opportunities that exist or are emerging within the South African development agenda.

In Kenya, our work is early in the design phase as we work out concrete details of technical assistance in support of our joint MOU with the Government of Kenya. Possible work may focus on support for the development of the renewable energy and energy efficiency master plan, support for design of policies that encourage adoption of renewable energy technologies including GOK feed in tariffs, assessments of grid reliability and ancillary services and requirements necessary for the Kenyan electricity grid to accept a greater share of variable renewable energy generation sources, and assistance to reduce barriers and increase private sector investment in renewable energy projects.

In Asia, the United States has established joint EC–LEDS work programs with Vietnam, Bangladesh, Indonesia, and Philippines. They are all in various stages of implementation, but the Philippines program is especially noteworthy for the speed at which it has advanced and the explicit links to constraints to economic growth.

The U.S. Government and the Philippines Government have agreed to a Partnership for Growth, which mobilizes the resources of both governments to address the most serious constraints to economic growth and development in the country, including hurdles in the energy and environment sectors. Building on this partnership, EC–LEDS will address two fundamental, constraints to growth: a pressing need for improved land use and resource planning that is integrated with both climate resiliency and development priorities; and, the lack of a consistent policy framework and reliable data for accelerating investment in domestic energy resources to ensure reliable, sustainable, and affordable energy access nationally.

The U.S. Government trained 29 Filipino technical experts on using the Long Range Energy Alternatives Planning System (LEAP) model to identify and prioritize climate change mitigation options. The next step is to develop and incorporate LEAP scenarios into the 2013 update of the Philippines Energy Plan. Another 35 transport and fuels analysts have been trained on tools and databases to analyze sustainable transport and fuel alternatives. Moving forward, USAID will support the development of high-quality that is essential to increasing wind development and private sector investment in utility-scale wind energy. This effort will benefit local industry, help to meet the country's clean energy growth target, and leverage 5MW of new RE generation in FY 2013.

USAID will also work to increase investment in wind and other renewable energy development by joining with the Asian Development Bank and the wind industry to provide training on overcoming barriers for wind development. This activity will result in increased investment in wind and other renewable energy development leading to $16M of new investment leveraged.

The U.S. Government is also helping the Government of Bangladesh integrate climate change goals with the country's broader economic development goals. For example, the USG is capitalizing on the linkages between climate change programming and the Feed the Future Initiative, which is promoting climate change adaptation through, for example, improved seeds and farm diversification, and greenhouse gas mitigation through techniques like improving fertilizer application techniques to reduce nitrogen emissions. Through the EC–LEDS program, the United States and Bangladesh are also partnering to help design and implement a low emission development strategy for Bangladesh. USAID specifically, is collecting data on wind energy potential and information on siting in order to unlock private investment in wind energy. We are also working with the Government of Bangladesh to build their capacity to manage and measure their own GHG emissions.

————

RESPONSES OF ADMINISTRATOR RAJIV SHAH TO QUESTIONS SUBMITTED
BY SENATOR BOB CORKER

FOOD AID REFORM

Question. Given USAID's statement that food aid reform will save an estimated $500 million over the next 10 years, are the savings identified by USAID going toward deficit reduction or toward other programming?

Answer. The President's proposal would use $500 million in savings generated from food aid reform to reduce the deficit. The shift of funding from title II to foreign assistance accounts eliminates mandatory funding for cargo preference reimbursements to title II, reducing the deficit by an estimated $50 million per year—$500 million over the next decade—based on recent data.

Question. How did the administration determine that 55 percent of the $1.4 billion food aid in guarantees will be spent in the United States? Why was that the final percentage?

Answer. The administration is committed to continuing a strong partnership with American farmers through the Food for Peace program. For that reason, the President's proposal maintains the majority of U.S. funds—55 percent in 2014—for the purchase, transport, and related costs of American commodities. This level is also based on our estimation of need and global market supply, taking into account the level of procurement local and regional markets can reasonably bear. That means the United States will keep working with farmers and processors across America who help feed hungry children from Bangladesh to the Sahel, where American commodities are the best possible tool. American farmers are vital to transforming the food aid basket with ready-to-use therapeutic foods, better fortification of blended foods, improved micronutrient reformulation for milled grains and vegetable oil, and emergency food bars and paste.

USAID FORWARD

Question. What controls has USAID established over its direct funding to local institutions to ensure accountability?

♦ Describe the mechanisms in place to respond to cases of inappropriate or inefficient use of funds.

◆ Have there been any cases where USAID has had to stop or pull back funding provided directly to local institutions? If so, please describe and provide some specific examples.

◆ Are the audit mechanisms and accountability standards for direct assistance to foreign governments the same as they are for U.S. recipients and other non-governmental recipients? If not, how do they differ?

Answer. USAID is committed to accountability, transparency, and oversight of USG funding and we have a number of mechanisms for ensuring that resources are not lost to waste, fraud, or abuse throughout development assistance implementation, as follows:

• *Pre-Award:* Contracting and Agreements Officers (CO/AO) make a determination whether a contractor/recipient is sufficiently responsible in terms of financial capabilities to account for funding, and have the ability to carry out or perform the work, under an award. This process is known as "a pre-award responsibility determination." As part of the Request for Proposal/Application process, CO/AOs also ensure that regulatory language enabling oversight and performance monitoring is included in each award. This language comes from the Federal Acquisition Regulation, the Office of Management and Budget (OMB) Circulars and/or Agency operational policy. Finally, performance indicators and metrics linked to the desired results are also included in the awards.

• *Post-Award:* During the period of performance for an award, USAID performs myriad activities to ensure award compliance. Contracting/Agreement Officer's Representatives COR/AORs review and approve awardee vouchers for invoices submitted, conduct site visits, and enable third-party program and project evaluations. They also monitor performance through reporting, meetings, and general oversight of the work being performed. COR/AORs formally document any material deficiencies in performance. This documentation triggers immediate action by an Agency CO/AO which may ultimately include recommending that the vendor not be paid. Additionally, we use financial systems and controls, as well as internal and independent audits to enable the Agency to effectively manage, track, and safeguard funds before they are disbursed.

• *Award Close-out:* Like other federal agencies, USAID uses the Contractor Performance Assessment Reporting System (CPARS) to formally record data about contractor performance. CORs are responsible for compiling and entering past performance data into CPARS annually. Additional USAID mechanisms are also in place to evaluate contractor performance including the post-performance audit process and the Office of the Inspector General to whom any instances of suspected waste, fraud, or abuse are promptly referred.

In February 2011, USAID stood up a Compliance Division within the Bureau for Management's Office of Acquisition and Assistance (M/OAA) to serve as the central repository for any and all referrals of administrative actions, including suspension and debarment actions. In just its first year the Division issued 102 administrative actions and recovered nearly $1 million. For this achievement the Agency was recognized by the Office of Management and Budget in 2012 as a success story:

> *"The Agency debarred 16 people in 2012 for their participation in a scheme to submit fraudulent receipts for the administration of federal foreign assistance to support public health, food aid, and disaster assistance in Malawi. By working with its recipient organization to assure that the unlawfully claimed funds were not reimbursed, USAID was able to avoid waste and abuse of taxpayer funds designed to provide vital assistance to a developing country."*—"Taking Contractor Accountability to the Next Level," September 18, 2012 (http://www.whitehouse.gov/blog/2012/09/18/taking-contractor-accountability-next-level).

With respect to audit mechanisms and accountability standards, U.S.-based grantees are subject to OMB Circular A–133 and U.S. contractors are subject to FAR 52.1215–2 and 52.216–7.

For all foreign-based recipient entity types, including contractors, grantees, and host government entities, audits are conducted in accordance with USAID Inspector General (IG) guidelines. The USAID IG guidelines were derived directly from U.S. Government auditing standards for implementation in the overseas, developing country context in which USAID financed performance takes place. The most notable difference between USAID audits on non-U.S. entities and U.S. entities is that a lower annual audit threshold is used for non-U.S. recipient entities—$300,000 in annual expenditures instead of the $500,000 threshold applicable by OMB to U.S. entities. Also, in most cases, foreign contractors and grantees and host governments are audited by independent, private sector auditors using the USAID IG guidelines.

59

However, pending USAID IG concurrence, audits on host government implementing entities may also be carried out by host government Supreme Audit Institutions. Such audits must comply with one of the following standards: (1) Comptroller General of the United States; (2) International Organization of Supreme Audit Institutions (INTOSAI); (3) International Auditing Practices Committee of the International Federation of Accountants (IFAC).

Question. According to the 2013 USAID Forward Progress Report, USAID increased the percentage of funding provided directly to local institutions from about 10 percent in FY 2010 [sic][1] to about 14 percent in FY 2012, with half going to partner country governments. Please describe what types of funding are included in this figure. For example, does the figure include funding provided through all assistance awards? Subawards?

Answer. The 14.3 percent figure referenced above (and from page 20 of the USAID Forward Progress report) represents the dollar value of cumulative mission program allocations[2] that were obligated through local systems during fiscal year 2012.

The figure includes all obligations at the mission level to partner country governments for direct implementation of assistance (projects) that involve direct use of previously assessed[3] partner country public financial management (including audit) and partner country procurement systems.

The figure also includes all direct funding through grants, cooperative agreements, contracts and Development Credit Authority mechanisms, to local, nongovernmental, nonprofit, educational, and commercial organizations. It does not include subawards such as subcontracts or subgrants. Local organizations are defined as entities organized and having a principal place of business in the recipient country, and majority owned or controlled by recipient country citizens, with less than a majority ownership or control by foreign entities or individuals.

Question. According to the 2013 USAID Forward Progress Report, USAID uses various tools to assess capacity and weaknesses of partner country government institutions and, in some cases, provides funding and assistance to these institutions. How many such assessments have been completed and in which countries?

Answer. As of March 2013, a total of 35 countries, listed below, have completed initial (''Stage One'') Public Financial Management Risk Assessment Framework (PFMRAF) assessments.

Armenia Bangladesh Barbados Benin Colombia Dominican Republic East Timor	El Salvador Ethiopia Georgia Ghana Haiti Honduras Indonesia	Jamaica Jordan Kenya Kosovo Liberia Malawi Mali	Moldova Morocco Mozambique Nepal Paraguay Peru Philippines	Rwanda Senegal Serbia South Africa Tanzania Trinidad and Tobago Zambia

Question. In how many (and which) countries is USAID providing funding directly to government institutions?

Answer. USAID is providing Direct Government-to-Government Assistance to the following 22 countries: Afghanistan, Kosovo, Armenia, Liberia, Benin, Mozambique, Bolivia, Nepal, Egypt, Pakistan, El Salvador, Peru, Ethiopia, Rwanda, Ghana, Senegal, Honduras, South Africa, India, Tanzania, Jordan, and Zambia.

Question. How do these assessments translate into USAID country assistance strategies and/or activities to build partner countries' public financial management capacity?

Answer. USAID's Country Development Cooperation Strategies (CDCS) are based on evidence and analysis, including that provided by the Public Financial Management Risk Assessment Framework (PFMRAF). At the strategy stage, the CDCS Guidance requires that the focus and selectivity principle be applied in selecting institutions and institutional levels (national, regional, local) which are most

[1] USAID has corrected the baseline year from 2012 as stated in the original QFR sent by Senator Corker, to 2010, to track the baseline year, FY 2010, established in USAID Forward Progress Report 2013.
[2] The term ''annual program allocation'' includes the missions' new obligating authority (NOA), carry-over funds, and transfers from other agencies (e.g., PEPFAR funds implemented by the mission; interagency transfers from State/DRL, State/INL).
[3] USAID's detailed assessment process for consideration of awards to partner country governments is described in QFRs 3, 5, and 8.

promising. Such a decision would be informed by a PFMRAF or other preliminary analysis.

After strategy approval, USAID's Project Design guidance requires a sustainability analysis to be performed. Missions are asked to analyze key sustainability issues and considerations around a host of issues including economic, financial, social soundness, cultural, institutional capacity, political economy, technical/sectoral, and environmental. Where appropriate, the analysis should discuss generally how funding local actors and supporting government-to-government objectives could help achieve sustainability goals. Further follow-on PFMRAF analysis of specific activities to support building country public financial management capacity may be conducted based on findings of the preliminary analysis.

For additional information regarding the Agency's CDCS guidance, please see: (http://www.usaid.gov/results-and-data/planning/country-strategies-cdcs).

Question. In 2012, GAO recommended that USAID develop a process to track assistance provided through local financial systems—in part to help monitor progress toward providing 30 percent of its assistance through these systems by 2015. Please update the committee on the status of USAID's efforts to develop such a process, including any changes made to USAID's accounting systems to capture this type of assistance.

Answer. While no changes were necessary to Agency core accounting or procurement systems, a process was developed by the Agency to track progress of providing assistance through local systems toward the goal of 30 percent of all country assistance programs by 2015. The process was part of a broader effort to track progress of all USAID Forward components which resulted in the publication of the USAID Forward Progress Report 2013. Annex 1 of the report, "Scorecard of Indicators," provides data for each goal reflecting the progress measure and 2012 milestone achieved. The report may be found at (http://www.usaid.gov/sites/default/files/documents/1868/2013-usaid-forward-report.pdf). Further, the Agency is working to refine and strengthen our reporting procedures to better integrate data collection with Agency standard business practices, improve data quality and more efficiently utilize existing technology.

Question. How did USAID determine that 30-percent target was a reasonable near term goal?

Answer. One of the key objectives of the Agency's reform effort, USAID Forward, is to increase the amount of work we do with more and varied local partners, so we can create true partnerships; build local, sustainable capacity; and begin to create the conditions where aid from the United States is no longer necessary.

The 30-percent "topline indicator" is an Agencywide aspirational target, not a mission-by-mission or country-by-country hard requirement. Every country in which USAID is operating has different levels of ministerial and local capacity, governance challenges, civil society participation and commitment to fight corruption, as well as a varying commitment to strengthen its systems and provide opportunities for local NGOs and private businesses.

USAID determined that the 30 percent overall target was a reasonable near term goal on the basis of USAID mission estimates (averaged to establish the overall target) of what progress toward localizing and increasing sustainability of assistance would be appropriate and prudent given the local context.

The selection of the implementing partner—whether a local government or nongovernmental organization, U.S. or international contractor or grantee, or other donors—is driven by country context and development needs, not by the 30 percent target.

For government-to-government assistance, USAID has an extensive assessment process in place that analyzes fiduciary risks and technical capacity, as well as the partner government's democracy, human rights, and governance record and capacity, before any decision is made to provide funding. Where manageable risks are identified, USAID implements a risk mitigation plan. If risk is too great, USAID chooses another approach.

For awards to local nongovernmental organizations, including local not-for-profit and commercial organizations, we also have an extensive process in place before any award to review a potential recipient's administrative, financial management and technical capacities to manage USAID funds and deliver results. USAID Agreement and Contracting officers must make a responsibility determination covering these factors before we provide funding or other resources.

Further, missions are instructed that partnership with local government entities or local organizations is not an end in itself. Rather, such partnerships should be the result of strategic planning, project design, identification of a development objective, and a determination of which modality among several—contracts and grants to U.S. or international organizations included—are the best fit for the project design and to achieve the development objective.

Whether it is government-to-government assistance or awards to local nongovernmental organizations, USAID always retains the unilateral right to suspend or terminate such assistance if any issues arise, and when necessary, USAID will seek to recover unallowable costs.

Question. How does USAID plan to measure performance [of awards to local organizations]? How does this differ from existing performance evaluation processes?

Answer. USAID has recently revised Agency guidance (the Automated Directive System) to the chapters covering strategic planning, project design, performance monitoring, and use of reliable partner government systems. An important reason for these updates was to ensure that USAID support for activities undertaken by partner governments or by local nongovernmental organizations were fully integrated into the Agency's established procedures for rigorous strategic planning, project design, and performance monitoring. Hence, awards to local organizations are subject to the same requirements for good project design and performance monitoring that applies to other awards that USAID makes. Good project design for all USAID projects includes development of a logical framework and associated performance indicators while good performance monitoring includes establishing a performance monitoring plan and conducting regular reviews.

Question. In 2012, GAO also recommended that USAID improve monitoring and evaluation of public financial management assistance programs. How is USAID monitoring and evaluating the effectiveness of efforts to use local systems, including identifying indicators and collecting data?

Answer. USAID Forward introduced two complementary reforms to address GAO's recommendation. The first effort reinvigorates strategy development and project design into USAID's development assistance programs. For the design of new projects, Agency requirements now include detailed preobligation analysis and indicative plans for monitoring progress and evaluation. This incorporates defining indicators, collecting baseline data, ensuring reliable results and planning for independent evaluations. Second, new guidance requires that final monitoring and evaluation plans include refined indicators and agreement on independent approaches to evaluation. These reforms are being incorporated into USAID's policy and directives systems for continuing use.

An important reason for updating the Agency's guidance is to ensure that activities undertaken by partner governments or by local nongovernmental organizations receiving USAID support are fully integrated into the Agency's established procedures for rigorous strategic planning, project design, performance monitoring, and evaluation. As such, all directly funded activities will be subject to the same requirements for good project design, performance monitoring and evaluation that apply to any other award that USAID would make. Good project design for all USAID projects includes development of a logical framework and associated performance indicators while good performance monitoring includes establishing a performance monitoring plan and conducting regular reviews.

Question. How does USAID coordinate its public financial management assistance activities with other USG agencies? With other donors?

Answer. USAID coordinated with the US. Department of the Treasury, the Millennium Challenge Corporation, other bilateral and multilateral donors, and international financial institutions before devising USAID's Public Financial Management Risk Assessment Framework (PFMRAF) assessment process. USAID's PFMRAF policy, set forth in our Automated Directives System Chapter 220, Use of Reliable Partner Country Systems for Direct Management and Implementation of Assistance, ordains a five stage assessment process to ensure that partner country government entities being considered as direct recipients of USAID funding have the appropriate financial, administrative, and technical capacities in place before USAID entrusts U.S. taxpayer funds to them.

USAID conducts these appraisals and assessments in person and in country, and invites and coordinates the participation of representatives of other executive branch agencies, other donors, and where appropriate, the potential partner country government. We also coordinate the provision of any technical assistance directed at enhancing public financial management capabilities of the partner governments via a country level interagency and donor coordination process. Finally, USAID has entered into interagency agreements with the Department of the Treasury and other U.S. Government agencies to provide technical assistance in the public financial management realm when these agencies have the resources and comparative advantage to do so, and when provision of such assistance furthers USAID's development objectives and project designs.

Question. What plans do you have to make available programmatic and expenditure data about assistance to host-country grantees and governments?

Answer. USAID intends to start publishing disaggregated program and expenditure data, including data fields at implementation level, on the Foreign Assistance Dashboard (FAD) after the close of the third quarter of FY 2013. The FAD provides a wide variety of stakeholders, both internal and external, with the ability to examine, research, and track U.S. Government foreign assistance investments in an accessible and easy-to-understand format. The disaggregation will also be applied retroactively to previously posted FY 2013 Quarters 1 and 2 data. Data fields that will be displayed include the name of the implementing agent (i.e., the organization, host country government or other entity that received the funding) and the implementing agent's country of origin.

TRADE CAPACITY

Question. U.S. development assistance should focus on helping developing nations achieve economic independence and graduate from U.S. assistance. Helping these countries attract investment and trade with the world is a critical part of achieving that goal. With respect to trade capacity-building (TCB), I am interested in (1) the administration's overall goals on trade capacity-building and (2) the specific strategy to coordinate the efforts of all the differing agencies providing trade capacity-building assistance.

◆ (a) What are the administration's top three goals with respect to trade capacity-building?

Answer. Through "aid for trade," the United States focuses on partnering with countries, particularly those countries that are least integrated into the global trading system, on training and technical assistance needed to: inform decisions about the benefits of trade arrangements and reforms; implement obligations to bring certainty to trade regimes; and enhance countries' ability to take advantage of the opportunities of the multilateral trading system and compete in a global economy. These goals are articulated in USAID's strategy document "Building Trade Capacity in the Developing World."

◆ (b) Please describe the interagency process by which all of the U.S. Government's agencies collaborate to set those goals and to construct a comprehensive strategy to implement those goals.

Answer. In the Presidential Policy Directive (PPD) on Global Development, the President laid out a modern architecture to raise the importance of development in our national security policymaking and to generate greater coherence across the U.S. Government. The PPD highlighted that "through existing policy mechanisms (e.g., trade policy through the United States Trade Representative's Trade Policy Review Group, etc.), an assessment of the "development impact of policy changes affecting developing countries will be considered." USTR chairs the interagency coordination process through the Trade Policy Review Group (TPRG) and the Trade Policy Staff Committee (TPSC). USAID has been using its position as a statutory member of this interagency process to inject the development impact and "on the ground" input from USAID field personnel into the trade policy decisionmaking apparatus, which includes discussions on the need for trade capacity-building interventions.

◆ (c) How does the interagency process identify and eliminate nontariff trade barriers?

Answer. USTR is responsible for annually publishing a National Trade Estimate Report on Foreign Trade Barriers (NTE). Information in this report is the result of input provided through the interagency TPSC process and supplemented by input in response to a notice published in the Federal Register, and by members of the private sector trade advisory committees and U.S. embassies abroad.

While the NTE identifies foreign trade barriers—efforts to eliminate them are led by USTR through a variety of negotiating avenues: bilaterally in direct discussion with trading partners; through regional bodies when they can play a significant role in addressing barriers across their member states; in multilateral negotiations; and, in some cases, through dispute settlement. USAID and other agencies which provide TCB often augment USTR's efforts by providing technical assistance in support of the policy changes necessary to eliminate nontariff barriers.

◆ (d) With respect to the administration's goals and the strategy on trade capacity-building, how do you define success?

Answer. The goal is to graduate countries from requiring U.S. foreign assistance. A number of former USAID-assisted countries have achieved that measure of success based on their strong economic and trade performance. Until that is achieved, the Department of State and USAID have worked together to develop standard indicators to measure what is being accomplished with foreign assistance resources, including indicators related to measuring the success of trade programs.

◆ (e) What are your criteria for success and how do you determine or measure your progress toward success?

Answer. A primary criterion for success of TCB programming is to expand the number of people that benefit from trade. This is accomplished through reducing the barriers that inhibit the flow of goods and services and working to integrate countries and businesses into the global trading system. In a 2005 study, the GAO raised questions about USG trade capacity-building efforts and the need for a more disciplined assessment of TCB interventions. As a result of that report, USAID undertook an extensive evaluation of TCB interventions and published a report of its findings in 2010. The study, "From Aid to Trade: Delivering Results" found that trade capacity-building had contributed substantially to achieving the goals of TCB. Individual USAID TCB projects also contain performance management plans which measure progress achieved under their respective programs. Evaluation of TCB programs and projects continues pursuant to USAID's evaluation policy.

◆ (f) What does a successful comprehensive trade capacity-building effort look like?

Answer. Integration into the global economy is a powerful force for economic growth and poverty reduction. The results of USAID trade capacity-building include more active and better informed participation by developing countries in a range of international trade negotiations, greater compliance with trade commitments and obligations, tangible improvements in the effectiveness of commercial laws and institutions, reduction in the time and cost to export and import goods, and improvements in the quantity and quality of individual developing country's exports, imports, and foreign investment. USAID has assisted more than 28 countries in acceding to the WTO. USAID assistance includes supporting the government in conducting analysis and preparing technical documents required for accession, as well as advice in undertaking required legal and regulatory reforms, and supporting effective implementation of those reforms.

◆ (g) Is there a specific country that you would describe as a success story?

Answer. Many countries which have received USAID trade capacity-building are considered success stories. For example, significant technical assistance and trade capacity building was provided as an integral part of the trade negotiations that led to the Dominican Republic-Central America-United States Free Trade Agreement (CAFTA–DR) with five Central American countries (Costa Rica, El Salvador, Guatemala, Honduras, and Nicaragua) and the Dominican Republic. U.S. TCB support to Vietnam over many years led to the successful implementation of the U.S.–Vietnam Bilateral Trade Agreement and subsequently, to Vietnam's accession to the World Trade Organization. USAID provided substantial assistance to Laos and Tajikistan to accede to the WTO in 2013.

Question. Our current budget environment demands that we spend scarce resources well. Please explain the administration's decision process to direct TCB aid to countries with the best chance of success. How do you decide where to spend TCB money to ensure it will do the most good? For example, under your comprehensive strategy, do you prioritize certain countries as being best positioned to implement the trade capacity-building aid we provide?

Answer. USAID works closely with USTR to identify U.S. trade policy priorities and to align USAID activities in support of those trade policy objectives. For example, USAID has implemented significant TCB programming to support implementation of U.S. trade agreements (CAFTA–DR, Peru, Colombia, Jordan, and Morocco) and utilization of trade preference programs such as the African Growth and Opportunity Act. In addition to working closely with USTR, USAID determines the need for trade capacity-building for individual countries through a Country Development Cooperation Strategy (CDCS) process that includes input from both U.S. and host country stakeholders and regional strategies that are developed through a Regional Development Cooperation Strategy (RDCS) process.

Question. A July 2011 GAO report notes that as many as 18 agencies provide trade capacity-building assistance. For example, the report identified that the Millennium Challenge Corporation and the Department of the Army as two of the largest providers of trade capacity-building assistance. Please describe the interagency process for coordinating decisionmaking with these other agencies and USAID's role in that process.

Answer. With respect to the Millennium Challenge Corporation, USAID serves on the MCC Board of Directors, along with the Departments of State and Treasury, and USTR. The Board is responsible for the identification and selection of MCC Threshold and Compact countries.

The Department of Defense is also a statutory member of the TPSC process led by USTR, through which trade-related policies are coordinated within the executive branch.

◆ (a) Does USAID lead the process?

Answer. The coordinating process for trade-policy-related issues is led by USTR. USAID works with USTR to identify TCB-related activities which complement U.S. trade policy goals. USAID is also part of the country team in U.S. embassies around the world. USAID works within the country team and with host country counterparts to identify and implement country specific trade capacity-building activities consistent with the partner country's development plan.

◆ (b) Can USAID direct the Army's efforts on where and how to spend trade capacity assistance?

Answer. USAID cannot direct the Army on where and how to spend trade capacity building assistance.

Question. The GAO has identified 18 agencies as providing trade capacity-building aid. Which U.S. Government agency is ultimately responsible to the President for ensuring that TCB aid is spent wisely and achieves the administration's goals as defined by the administration's overall trade capacity-building strategy?

Answer. USAID works with USTR and other agencies as appropriate to align USAID TCB programs to support trade policy and broader USG objectives.

◆ (a) Which agency and which official is in charge of the process that decides where U.S. trade capacity-building money will be directed?

Answer. There is no single coordinating agency, official, or process specific to TCB activities. USAID, as the largest provider of TCB assistance, coordinates closely with USTR, State, Treasury, Agriculture, Labor and other trade related agencies in prioritizing TCB efforts. USAID programs identify TCB needs through a Country Development Cooperation Strategy (CDCS) process that includes input from both U.S. and host country stakeholders and regional strategies that are developed through a Regional Development Cooperation Strategy (RDCS) process. These strategies are approved by the cognizant USAID regional Assistant Administrator with input from USAID policy, budget, and technical bureaus.

◆ (b) Can that agency and that official direct how resources are spent?

Answer. There is no single agency or individual that directs how all TCB resources are spent.

◆ (c) Which of the 18 agencies officially participate in that process?

Answer. Most of the USG entities that provide TCB are statutory members of the TPSC interagency process led by USTR such as the Departments' of Agriculture, Commerce, Defense, Energy, Health and Human Services, Homeland Security, Interior, Justice, Labor, State, Transportation, Treasury, the Environmental Protection Agency and USAID.

◆ (d) According to the President's Congressional Budget Justification, some of this money is being spent to help foreign governments modernize customs procedures at foreign ports. For example, is reducing delays and paperwork at ports one of the established benchmarks for success?

Answer. USAID focuses significant attention to the issue of trade facilitation, particularly reducing the time and cost to move goods. USAID trade facilitation activities include active support for customs and border management reforms at border crossings, ports, and along major transit corridors. In addition, USAID has worked closely with USTR to support the WTO negotiations on a Trade Facilitation Agreement. In particular, USAID recently launched the Partnership for Trade Facilitation, which is working with 17 countries to respond quickly to requests for assistance from trade and customs authorities for help with implementing aspects of the proposed WTO agreement on trade facilitation. Additional efforts to improve trade facilitation are also being carried out by USAID's Africa trade hubs to promote both United States-Africa trade as well as intra-African trade. Specific indicators tracked in many USAID trade facilitation projects include the time, number of procedures and cost (including informal payments) to clear goods through customs and border agencies or to move goods along major transit corridors.

◆ (e) How do you identify, with the help of the business community, specific areas where aid could be best applied?

Answer. USAID's country and regional development strategies are primarily developed by its field missions, which seek input from host country private sector stakeholders. USAID/Washington also plays an active role in the development of these assistance strategies and contributes input that reflects U.S. private sector views and concerns as identified by USTR through its statutory private sector consultative process—the Trade Advisory Committee system.

◆ (f) What is the process for seeking their input?

Answer. In 1974, Congress created the trade advisory committee system to ensure that U.S. trade policy and trade negotiating objectives adequately reflect U.S. public and private sector interests. The advisory committee system consists of 28 advisory committees, with a total membership of approximately 700 citizen advisors.

USTR's Office of Intergovernmental Affairs & Public Engagement (IAPE) manages the advisory committees, in cooperation with other agencies, including the Departments of Agriculture, Commerce, and Labor, and the Environmental Protection Agency.

AFGHANISTAN/DEVELOPMENT IN WAR ZONES AND CONTINGENCIES

Question. The Special Inspector General for Afghanistan Reconstruction (SIGAR) estimates that there is about $10 billion in assistance given to Afghanistan annually, yet the government raises only about $2 billion in revenue. In your estimate, what is the gap between foreign assistance flowing into Afghanistan to start and maintain reconstruction and stabilization projects and the revenue the Government of Afghanistan can be expected to accumulate in a given year? What is the plan to overcome this challenge going forward?

Answer. The World Bank estimates the financing gap could reach as high as 40 percent of the Afghan Government's budget in 2017 (including security costs), then drop to around 25 percent in 2021 assuming an increase in mining revenues. The current financing gap is estimated at 5.3 percent of GDP (2012), which continues to be financed entirely by donor grants. The fiscal sustainability ratio, defined as the percentage of operating expenses covered by domestic revenues—was 59 percent for FY 2012. Domestic revenues financed approximately 40 percent of the operating budget and the development expenditures.

In 2011, the Ministry of Finance reported that the Government of Afghanistan collected more than $2 billion in revenues for the first time ever, representing more than a 140-percent increase since 2008. Customs accounted for about 48 percent of the revenues. Domestic revenues increased by 7 percent in 2012, reaching US$2.15 billion. The World Bank reported that the Afghan Government expects domestic revenues to increase to US$2.5 billion (11.6 percent of GDP) this year, with increases in all sources of revenue. This could finance approximately 65 percent of the operating expenditures, with the remainder to be financed through donor grants.

Donors have committed to cover the financing gap for several years. Pledges from all donors at the July 2012 donor meeting in Tokyo totaled $16 billion in development aid to Afghanistan over 4 years. Together with earlier pledges on the security side, annual aid would amount to about $8 billion—divided roughly equally between civil and security aid.

USAID is continuing to work with the Government of Afghanistan and the international donor community to improve trade, strengthen customs, and support the Ministry of Mines in managing natural resource extractions. In addition, USAID's agriculture strategy is focused both on food security and high-value exports. These efforts are supporting the Government of Afghanistan in growing its public revenue and manage expenditures so it can better manage its own financing needs.

Question. In its final report, the Special Inspector General for Iraq Reconstruction concluded that: "The U.S. Government is not much better prepared for the next stabilization operation than it was in 2003." Do you agree with that assessment? If not, why not?

◆ (a) As a government, do we require a different approach to planning and implementation in reconstruction and stabilization circumstances?

◆(b) Are structural changes needed at USAID, in the interagency coordination structures, or within specific programs?

Answer. We respectfully defer to the Department of State's Office of Civilian Response (CSO) to address the broader question of the U.S Government's ability to respond to a stabilization initiative. CSO, formerly known as the Civilian Reconstruction and Stabilization Office (S/CRS), was specifically created in 2004 in the aftermath of Iraq.

As to USAID's readiness, since 2004 a number of structural changes have better positioned the Agency to successfully support stabilization type operations. One such change includes the creation of USAID's Office of Conflict Management and Mitigation which, among other things, developed a Conflict Assessment Framework (CAF) in 2005 to better understand the underlying causes of conflict and instability in a country or region. The CAF has been updated to reflect a more nuanced understanding of these causes and has been used repeatedly by our missions in the development of new projects and strategies. Agency staff has been trained in the use of the CAF as well as other conflict-related subjects, making USAID staff both in Washington and in the field, more capable of designing programs and applying our development assistance support to stabilization objectives.

In 2005, USAID launched a comprehensive human capital strategic planning process which identified the lack of depth in critical core areas such as education, health, and agriculture, and concluded that this was severely constraining the Agency's ability to "surge" staff in support of pre- and post-conflict programs in Iraq and other Critical Priority Countries around the world. Staffing shortages were limiting USAID's direct engagement with foreign government agencies and local partners. Subsequently, USAID implemented an ambitious hiring effort, the Development Leadership Initiative (DLI), paralleling the Department of State's Diplomacy 2.0 Initiative, with bipartisan congressional support and increased funding. Since 2008, USAID has recruited approximately 800 additional Foreign Service officers through the DLI program who now constitute part of USAID's ranks of technical specialists. Since 2010, eight DLIs have served or are serving in Iraq and 50 DLIs have served or are serving in Afghanistan. An increase in Foreign Service officers has better positioned USAID to meet our technical staffing needs abroad.

Many lessons learned from the Iraq have been incorporated into USAID's development assistance, including:

• Define what is needed for sustainability from the start by ensuring that the host country beneficiaries are involved in setting priorities and developing the capacities within their societies to lead their own development. In some cases, the host country was not involved in the planning stage of an activity and the activity was less successful.
• Ensure that people sent overseas to support a mission or program possess the appropriate skills and experience.
• The duration of the tour is critical to ensuring the sustainability and continuity of programs.

An example of where USAID has incorporated sustainability into its programming is Iraqi Government cost-sharing. Over the past year, the Iraqi Government, through several Memoranda of Understanding, has committed to cost share important USAID activities. This demonstrates both the Iraqis' willingness to pursue critical development objectives and invest their own resources into their own development. This has enabled USAID to redirect resources to strengthen Iraqi governing institutions, promote private sector development, and assist vulnerable populations such as ethnic and religious minorities, internally displaced persons, female-headed households and youth.

In Afghanistan, all projects, both current and planned, must undergo an analysis to determine (1) Afghan ownership; (2) cost/program effectiveness; and (3) contributions to stability. Through the Accountable Assistance for Afghanistan (A3) initiative, USAID is carrying out a 100-percent audit of all locally incurred costs, expanding monitoring and evaluation capacity to include hundreds of USAID onsite monitors in the field, and has placed limits on the number of subcontractor tiers.

HOST NATION RECONSTRUCTION/INFRASTRUCTURE SUSTAINABILITY

Question. How does USAID collect and record information from nations receiving U.S. foreign aid about their abilities to pay for the maintenance or expansion of infrastructure we have funded?

Answer. USAID receives and analyzes information regarding recipient nations' ability to pay for the maintenance or expansion of U.S. foreign aid funded infrastructure construction activities through the completion of a Foreign Assistance Act of 1961 Section 611(e) certification process. When a capital assistance project is proposed, and total U.S. assistance for it will exceed $1 million, the Mission Director must review and certify a country's capability to effectively maintain and utilize the assistance. Pursuant to section 611(e), the certification is then forwarded to the cognizant Assistant Administrator, as delegated by the Administrator, for consideration. During project design, an analysis of the capital cost and operation and maintenance costs along with an analysis of host country technical and financial capability to operate and maintain capital projects is undertaken. The project design includes training and institutional reform components to increase the capability of the host country to operate and maintain the facility that is being financed, and often continues after the facility is constructed.

Question. What policies and procedures does USAID have in place to prevent the funding of projects that, when added to the aggregate of USAID projects in the same country, would be beyond the capability of the host nation to raise sufficient resources domestically to maintain the work that we have funded?

Answer. As part of USAID Forward reform efforts to strengthen the Agency's project design process, all missions must complete a mandatory sustainability analysis that assesses the host country's ability to sustain the development gains that would be achieved through the project. The sustainability analysis should include a review of the financial implications of the project. For any organization to be sustained following completion of the project (whether governmental or nongovernmental), a recurrent cost analysis must be undertaken that estimates the costs of operations during the project and of continuing expected functions at the end of the project and estimated sources of revenue. The recurrent cost analysis should take into consideration maintenance capability and all other costs anticipated to implement the project activities, business operations or infrastructure on a continuing or recurring basis.

HIRING VETS

Question. The most recent version of the Office of Personnel Management report on federal veteran employment claims that just 7.2 percent of USAID employees are veterans, making the agency the third-lowest in the executive branch for percentage of veterans on staff. Given that many of our veterans' experience in contingency environments seem to match exactly with the current needs of USAID programs still ongoing in contingency environments, what do you think contributes to such low levels of veterans in the ranks of USAID employees?

Answer. Veterans have greatly contributed to the Agency and work in myriad professional and administrative positions in the United States and overseas. There has been a significant increase in USAID's data on veterans since the issuance of the OPM report. Currently, there are 356 veterans employed at USAID (9.3 percent of the Agency's total workforce). Indeed, veterans account for 14.6 percent of the Agency's Civil Service employees (251 veterans) and 4.9 percent of our Foreign Service staff (105 veterans). In addition, the Agency is trending well above its FY 2013 veteran hiring goals of 15.3 percent for veteran new hires and 4.7 percent for disabled veterans. As of May 2013, 24 percent of USAID's new hires were veterans and 6 percent have been disabled veterans. As discussed in response to the Question below, the Agency will continue its efforts to increase the number of veterans in the Agency.

Question. Beyond that mandated by the President's Veterans Employment Initiative, has USAID implemented any additional programming for veterans?

Answer. USAID has implemented a number of aggressive strategies to increase the number of veterans in the Agency. We began by hiring a full-time employee as our Veteran Employment Program Manager. The Program Manager has initiated a robust referral program that targets veterans for vacancies as soon as they occur. The referral program has allowed veterans to be referred for consideration prior to the posting of a job announcement. As a result, 30 percent of all veterans hired in FY12 were referred from this highly successful program. In addition, USAID sponsors quarterly Federal Employment Workshops at our headquarters, at no cost, for separating and retiring military members and spouses. We have also increased the number of veterans hired through our formal Student Internship Program, as well as by partnering with a wide variety of Military Transition Assistance Programs and Veterans Rehabilitation Organizations.

Question. As USAID continues to have significant involvement in contingency zones, its projects demand exceptional leadership and character on the part of

USAID personnel. Have veterans enabled USAID to more effectively carry out contingency missions?

Answer. Our veterans' previous military experience has allowed them to transition directly into positions conducting development and diplomacy in contingency zones and other locales. For example, during FY12, USAID hired 13 veterans as Foreign Service Limited Officers to work on critical priority programs in Afghanistan, Pakistan, and Yemen. Their work has indeed enabled the Agency to be effective in carrying out its mission.

Question. By virtue of their service, veterans bring a unique and valued perspective to any government agency. In what ways do you think an increase in veteran employment at USAID would have on the culture of USAID?

Answer. Veterans hired by USAID have contributed greatly to our mission. Their discipline, work ethic, and leadership skills, coupled with the USAID-specific technical skills they have learned, make them well suited for a variety of positions at USAID. Veterans at the Agency are currently working in occupations such as acquisition, information technology, communications, security, human resources, engineering, public policy, finance, and education.

Question. Please describe any specific plans you have to increase the hiring of veterans by USAID.

Answer. USAID will continue to implement a number of strategies to increase the number of veterans in the Agency. Specifically, we will continue to increase veteran hiring by improving the following:

- Continue to sponsor USAID Federal Employment Workshops onsite at no cost for separating/retiring military and spouses;
- Support the Operation Warfighter and Wounded Warrior Programs;
- Continue to develop our partnership with the Department of Veterans Affairs Vocational Rehabilitation & Employment Program;
- Increase the number of veterans hired as interns through the Pathways Program;
- Expand the Agency Veterans Hiring Database and usage of OPM's Shared Database of People With Disabilities
- Continue to participate in Military Transition Assistance Programs (TAP); and
- Increase hiring of veterans through the Foreign Service Junior Officer Program. This vital program brings qualified applicants into the Agency's Foreign Service to assume positions of increasing responsibility for planning, implementing, and managing USAID's economic and humanitarian assistance programs.

CLIMATE CHANGE

Question. USAID's budget fact sheet states that $481 million is requested for the Global Climate Change Initiative "implemented in partnership with the Department of State." Of this, how much funding is requested for USAID?

Answer. Of the $481 million request for the Global Climate Change Initiative in partnership with the Department of State, $349 Million is being requested for USAID.

Question. What dollar amount of FY 2014 USAID climate change funding is going to the United Nations and affiliated agencies? How much was provided in FY 2012?

Answer. It is too early to tell how much USAID climate change funding may be implemented through United Nations (U.N.) programs in FY 2014. In FY 2012, USAID did not provide direct climate change funding to United Nations agencies or programs.

Question. In the past 10 years, how much climate change funding has USAID spent on programming for peer-to-peer interaction and information-sharing (e.g., conferences, Web sites, exchanges, fellowship, etc.)? What specific advances have been made in U.S. development goals through these types of initiatives?

Answer. Addressing climate change depends on having the best available data and tools and knowing how to apply them. USAID has made this type of assistance a priority to help expand the knowledge base and more broadly and effectively share information. Several of our approaches to climate assistance have been delivered through the types of mechanisms that you reference, particularly peer-to-peer knowledge-sharing and information-exchanges.

For example, SERVIR Global, USAID's partnership with NASA, works with scientists and decision makers around the world to provide training and access to satellite and geospatial data and applications. These applications are being used to predict a range of natural hazards, from red tide blooms in El Salvador to stream flows in Kenya to forest fires in the Himalaya region. Over the past 10 years, USAID has programmed approximately $29 million, with NASA also providing approximately $22.4 million, to develop and sustain this information sharing tool. In 2011, the Environment Minister for El Salvador estimated that the red tide information available from SERVIR averted $14 million in losses. In Africa, SERVIR has developed early warning tools for Rift Valley Fever, a vector-borne disease. In an effort to increase evidence-based decisionmaking among countries, USAID is expanding this partnership in west Africa and Central Asia in FY 2013.

USAID does not distinctly capture these approaches collectively as an indicator or reporting category within climate funding.

Question. What are the overall objectives of the climate change programs? What are specific outcomes (not outputs) USAID aims to achieve? How will you measure progress and determine success or failure?

Answer. USAID's 2012 Climate Change and Development Strategy defines three objectives: (1) reducing greenhouse gas emissions by accelerating targeted countries' transition to low emission development through clean energy and sustainable landscape use (mitigation); (2) increasing the resilience of people, places and livelihoods to climate change (adaptation); and (3) integrating climate change considerations into USAID's programs, policies and operations (integration).

Regarding outcomes and related measures, USAID assistance is refining the development of a series of indicators against which we will assess the success of our climate change programming. For example, USAID will assess: (1) whether assisted countries prepare greenhouse gas inventories and sustain the quality of those inventories; (2) whether partner countries' national and subnational development plans are informed by climate change analysis and include mitigation and/or adaptation actions; (3) the extent to which stakeholders are using climate information in their decisionmaking; and (4) tracking increased leverage of public and private sector investment devoted to climate change mitigation and adaptation as a result of USG assistance.

USAID is engaging in an organized effort with other donor and implementing agencies to explore ways to assess the capacity of individuals, households, and institutions to adapt to climate change. With the help of evaluations, such analysis will allow for the assessment of impact of adaptation assistance in post-disaster situations, as well as create opportunities to strengthen the predictive quality of the outcome measures outlined above.

––––––––

RESPONSES OF ADMINISTRATOR RAJIV SHAH TO QUESTIONS SUBMITTED
BY SENATOR BARBARA BOXER

GENDER-BASED VIOLENCE STRATEGY AND INDIA

Question. It is my understanding that you traveled to India last month to focus, at least in part, on violence against women. So I am certain that you are aware of the heartbreaking stories that have emerged out of India recently, including the gang rape of a 23-year-old woman on a bus last December. Her injuries were so horrific that she later died of them. A Swiss tourist was also gang raped by five men while traveling with her husband. And just last week, a 5-year-old girl was kidnapped, repeatedly raped, and nearly killed. These cases—as well as others—have garnered significant international attention and sparked protests within India.

◆ How is USAID working in India to help address rape and other forms of gender-based violence?
◆ Is there more that we could be doing, especially in light of the recently announced U.S. Strategy to Prevent and Respond to Gender-Based Violence Globally?

Answer. USAID shares your strong concern about gender-based violence and violence against children in India.

Our approach in India and other countries around the world is to work across sectors to identify and close gender gaps wherever they exist, because we recognize the broader benefits that arise when women are able to realize their rights and determine their own outcomes. USAID/India's goal is to enhance women's leadership and gender equality in all program sectors in which we work, including health, clean energy, and agriculture programs, and identify entry points in each of these sectors to address gender-based violence and other barriers to gender equality.

In India, we are working through a variety of partnership mechanisms to identify innovative approaches to combating gender-based violence (GBV) that build on local knowledge, Indian innovation, and show the potential for scale and replication in India and around the world.

USAID is partnering with Care, ITVS—the independent television station, and the Ford Foundation to support Women and Girls Lead Global. In India, this program is working to engage men and boys and change their attitudes and behaviors related to GBV. USAID is partnering with U.N. Women to implement the Safe Cities program in New Delhi—an innovative program that employs a gender empowerment approach to the issue of urban planning and infrastructure development. The goal is for girls and women to reclaim their right to public spaces. Further, we are working through our health programming in India to identify entry points in patient care where front line health workers are equipped in a systematic way to identify GBV in patients as well as counsel them and refer them for care.

The U.S. Strategy to Prevent and Respond to Gender-Based Violence Globally is a milestone in solving this critical problem and USAID has developed an implementation plan to realize the goals of the strategy, yet there is always more to be done. USAID appreciates the efforts and coordination of many U.S. Government agencies at home and abroad to implement this strategy as well as the advocacy from senior leadership across the government.

MALALA YOUSAFZAI AND PAKISTAN

Question. Earlier this year, I introduced the Malala Yousafzai Scholarship Act with Senator Landrieu. Specifically, it would build upon an existing USAID-funded scholarship program for disadvantaged Pakistani students by increasing the number of scholarships awarded each year by 30 percent and requiring that all of these new scholarships be awarded to women. To date, only 25 percent of the program's scholarships have gone to women.

- ◆ Will you commit to working with me to ensure that Pakistani women are given full and equal access to USAID scholarship programs?
- ◆ What more can the United States do to expand educational opportunities for women and girls in Pakistan and around the world?

Answer. USAID is committed to ensuring that Pakistani women are given full and equal access to USAID-funded scholarship programs. USAID specifically supports the goal of increasing the number of scholarships available to Pakistani women under USAID's Merit and Needs-Based Scholarship Program (MNBSP). The MNSBP provides scholarships for Pakistani students to attend bachelor's and master's degree programs at Pakistani universities, targeting underserved populations, including women.

Based on an overall positive independent evaluation of the MNBSP issued in August 2012, USAID is making several programmatic adjustments to reach that goal. These adjustments are scheduled to take effect for university enrollment in September 2013. Among these adjustments are targeting of the distribution of scholarships to women for entrance into the fall 2013 matriculation at 50 percent; this is 4 percent above the ratio of women attending university as a percentage of the university-going population (46 percent). In order to reach the 50 percent target, USAID is expanding disciplines of study from agriculture and business to a wide variety of fields popular with women from chemical engineering to journalism. USAID is also expanding the university pool to include five women's universities. In addition, in our other scholarship programs in Pakistan, we have set a 50 percent target for scholarship awards to women.

Scholarship programs are only one aspect of USAID's education initiative in Pakistan. In many areas parents will only send their girls to schools with an all-female teaching staff, so increasing the number of women teaching will expand access to education for girls. To ensure more girls have the opportunity to pursue basic education, USAID is working to mobilize communities to increase girls' enrollment in school and training female teachers, which encourages families to send their girls to school. USAID is also constructing or rehabilitating over 185 girls' schools in Sindh, FATA, Khyber Pakhtunkhwa, and Balochistan. To address the challenges of educational quality, which impacts access, USAID will be transforming the way classroom teachers teach and assess reading over the next 5 years by working with universities and colleges on new degree programs in preservice teacher education as well as working with in-service teachers.

Similarly, USAID is working to expand opportunities for women and girls worldwide. In 2012, the Agency adopted a new policy on Gender Equality and Female Empowerment, which includes equal access to education as part of its vision. Among the requirements under this new policy are that gender equality and female empowerment must be integrated throughout the program cycle: in policy and strategy formation, project design and implementation, and monitoring and evaluation. USAID's Automated Directives System, which dictates operational policy, also requires gender analyses to guide long-term planning and project design so that men and women experience an equal opportunity to benefit from and contribute to economic, social, cultural, and political development; enjoy socially valued resources and rewards; and realize their human rights.

Taken together, these efforts along with those that the Agency has undertaken around the National Action Plan on Women, Peace and Security, preventing Gender-Based Violence, ending Child Marriage and Countering-Trafficking in Persons, provide a global approach for the empowerment of women.

CLIMATE CHANGE

Question. Numerous statements and studies from the defense and national security communities have warned that climate change and its impacts—from extreme events to sea-level rise to water and food scarcity—will create political instability, especially in the poorest and least able to adapt countries.

◆ How will funding the President's budget request for the Department of State and USAID's efforts on global climate change help prevent and mitigate such impacts and assist U.S. national security priorities?

Answer. Global climate change has the potential to significantly alter the relationships between people and their environment. It could undermine the resource base upon which people have built their livelihoods and sociopolitical institutions. However, there remains little certainty over exactly how these changes will be manifested in specific events and locations and what the consequences will be in terms of economic development, political stability, peace and security. It has therefore become a priority for USAID to help build an evidence base about the relationship between climate, resources, and conflict and to be able to knowledgeably inform both development policy and programming, especially when working in fragile and conflict affected areas.

USAID recognizes at least three ways by which climate change could potentially contribute to armed conflict or violent social unrest: (1) climate change could intensify existing environmental or resource problems (whether due to scarcity or abundance); (2) climate change could create new environmental problems that contribute to instability; and (3) the introduction of climate-related resources and financing could interact with existing grievances and fault lines in counterproductive or destructive ways.

USAID and other development organizations have recognized these risks and have widely accepted the need to be ''conflict-sensitive'' in climate-related interventions. The FY14 foreign assistance request includes funds for the collection of needed data and for adaptation funding as a critical component of the climate change program.

We believe our adaptation programs will play a critical role in helping prevent and mitigate instability caused by the impacts of climate change. USAID adaptation programs seek to make early and smart investments to build the resilience of vulnerable communities and reduce many of the negative impacts of climate change. Adaptation funds are targeted at the poorest and most vulnerable countries, both in terms of exposure to physical impacts of climate change and socioeconomic sensitivity to those impacts. USAID's Climate Change and Development Strategy prioritizes small island developing states, glacier-dependent nations, and least developed countries, especially in Africa, for adaptation investment. The Global Climate Change Initiative is a critical component of USAID's Resilience Strategy; considering the current and future effects of climate change allows us not only to better predict, prepare for, and respond to shocks and stresses (e.g., hurricanes, flooding, and droughts) but also to improve planning for the long-term stresses of climate change.

Question. As we have seen here in the United States, extreme weather events associated with climate change are increasing in their number and impact. The frequency and intensity of these events will only increase. The poor and countries least able to adapt are the most vulnerable to extreme events and other climate change impacts such as sea-level rise, water and food scarcity, and shifting seasons and disease vectors.

◆ How will funding the President's budget request for the Department of State and USAID's global climate change efforts help prevent and mitigate the impacts of climate change on the world's most vulnerable people and nations?

Answer. FY 2014 adaptation funding will bolster the Global Climate Change Initiative's efforts to increase the resilience of vulnerable communities to climate threats, and preserve hard-won development gains in democracy, food security, health, economic growth, and natural resource management. Through adaptation programming, the United States is contributing to stability and sustainable economic growth in developing countries, preventing loss of life, and reducing the need for post-disaster assistance.

With FY 2014 resources, USAID will support on-the-ground programs that rigorously test the effectiveness of adaptation actions, disseminate lessons learned and catalyze their widespread adoption to build resilience across communities, countries, and regions. Adaptation funding will also be used to support strategic investments in science and analysis for decisionmaking, and tools and platforms that can be used in multiple countries around the world. For example, USAID will continue to extend climate forecasting technology systems, such as the Famine Early Warning System and SERVIR, to help vulnerable countries adapt and respond to shocks.

- The USAID-supported Famine Early Warning System Network (FEWS NET) is an information system designed to identify problems in the food supply system that potentially lead to famine or other food-insecure conditions in sub-Saharan Africa, Afghanistan, Central America, and Haiti. The USGS FEWS NET Data Portal provides access to geospatial data, satellite image products, and derived data products in support of FEWS NET monitoring needs throughout the world. This portal is provided by the USGS FEWS NET Project, part of the Early Warning and Environmental Monitoring Program at the USGS Earth Resources Observation and Science (EROS) Center. (http://early.warning-usgs.gov/fews/index.php) FEWS NET predicted a recent drought in Africa and allowed donors to take quick action before the worst conditions set in. In those areas that were expected to be hit the hardest, USAID helped households with "commercial destocking"—selling off some livestock while the prices were still high, which helped families bring in enough income to feed themselves and their remaining livestock. USAID also prepositioned significant amounts of food and nonfood commodities and worked to rehabilitate wells before the worst drought conditions, preventing the need to launch expensive water trucking efforts in those regions.

In Mozambique, USAID will help vulnerable coastal cities incorporate climate change projections into their planning processes and implement adaptation measures to reduce risks associated with sea-level rise, flooding, storms, and erosion; direct beneficiaries will include municipal governments, local communities, nongovernmental organizations, and faith-based organizations. In the Dominican Republic, USAID will build on a new partnership with reinsurer Swiss Re to make an affordable tailored weather index insurance product commercially available to small farmers who are currently unable to make optimal productive investments due to increasing risks of drought or flooding. Hundreds of Dominican farmers will also receive training and technical assistance on climate change, financial management, and the design and application of farm-level risk reduction measures. USAID has built an impact evaluation around this project in the Dominican Republic, and will be gathering evidence of the effectiveness of this holistic risk management approach over the next 2 to 4 years.

USAID programs will also promote effective governance for climate change adaptation, by helping governments integrate climate resilience into development planning, and building the capacity of civil society organizations and the private sector to engage in policymaking processes.

Adaptation resources will be spent in the vulnerable countries and communities that need them most. The Global Climate Change Initiative prioritizes adaptation funding for least developed countries, especially in sub-Saharan Africa, small-island developing states, and glacier-dependent countries.

RESPONSES OF ADMINISTRATOR RAJIV SHAH TO QUESTIONS SUBMITTED
BY SENATOR RON JOHNSON

Question. Foreign assistance is an important component of America's foreign and defense policy. I am proud of the fact that we portray American values around the world, and when done effectively and strategically, it is money well spent. At the same time, however, we have a responsibility to ensure that taxpayer funds are being spent in the national interest, and our allies and partners have not always been reliable. The American public has become more skeptical of aid, and in some cases, with good reason.

◆ In your opinion, what is the best way of holding accountable recipients of U.S. assistance, while also understanding the reality of difficult situations, whether discussing Egypt, Pakistan, Syria or others?

Answer. USAID is committed to accountability, transparency, and oversight of USG funding and we have a number of mechanisms for ensuring that resources are not lost to waste, fraud, or abuse throughout development assistance implementation, as follows:

- *Pre-Award:* Contracting and Agreements Officers (CO/AO) make a determination whether a contractor/recipient is sufficiently responsible in terms of financial capabilities to account for funding, and have the ability to carry out or perform the work, under an award. This process is known as "a pre-award responsibility determination." As part of the Request for Proposal/Application process, CO/AOs also ensure that regulatory language enabling oversight and performance monitoring is included in each award. This language comes from the Federal Acquisition Regulation, the Office of Management and Budget (OMB) Circulars and/or Agency operational policy. Finally, performance indicators and metrics linked to the desired results are also included in the awards.

- *Post-Award:* During the period of performance for an award, USAID performs myriad activities to ensure award compliance. Contracting/Agreement Officer's Representatives COR/AORs review and approve awardee vouchers for invoices submitted, conduct site visits, and enable third-party program and project evaluations. They also monitor performance through reporting, meetings, and general oversight of the work being performed. COR/AORs formally document any material deficiencies in performance. This documentation triggers immediate action by an Agency CO/AO which may ultimately include recommending that the vendor not be paid. Additionally, we use financial systems and controls, as well as internal and independent audits to enable the Agency to effectively manage, track, and safeguard funds before they are disbursed.

- *Award Close-out:* Like other federal agencies, USAID uses the Contractor Performance Assessment Reporting System (CPARS) to formally record data about contractor performance. CORs are responsible for compiling and entering past performance data into CPARS annually. Additional USAID mechanisms are also in place to evaluate contractor performance including the post-performance audit process and the Office of the Inspector General to whom any instances of suspected waste, fraud, or abuse are promptly referred.

In February 2011, USAID stood up a Compliance Division within the Bureau for Management's Office of Acquisition and Assistance (M/OAA) to serve as the central repository for any and all referrals of administrative actions, including suspension and debarment actions. In just its first year the Division issued 102 administrative actions and recovered nearly $1 million. For this achievement the Agency was recognized by the Office of Management and Budget in 2012 as a success story:

> *"The Agency debarred 16 people in 2012 for their participation in a scheme to submit fraudulent receipts for the administration of federal foreign assistance to support public health, food aid, and disaster assistance in Malawi. By working with its recipient organization to assure that the unlawfully claimed funds were not reimbursed, USAID was able to avoid waste and abuse of taxpayer funds designed to provide vital assistance to a developing country."*—"Taking Contractor Accountability to the Next Level," September 18, 2012 (http://www.whitehouse.gov/blog/2012/09/18/taking-contractor-accountability-next-level).

With respect to audit mechanisms and accountability standards, U.S.-based grantees are subject to OMB Circular A–133 and U.S. contractors are subject to FAR 52.1215–2 and 52.216–7. For all foreign-based recipient entity types, including contractors, grantees and host government entities, audits are conducted in accordance with USAID Inspector General (IG) guidelines. The USAID IG guidelines were derived directly from U.S. Government auditing standards for implementation in the overseas, developing country context in which USAID financed performance takes place. The most notable difference between USAID audits on non-U.S. entities and U.S. entities is that a lower annual audit threshold is used for non-U.S. recipient entities—$300,000 in annual expenditures instead of the $500,000 threshold applicable by OMB to U.S. entities. Also, in most cases, foreign contractors and grantees and host governments are audited by independent, private sector auditors using the USAID IG guidelines. However, pending USAID IG concurrence, audits on host government implementing entities may also be carried out by host government Supreme Audit Institutions. Such audits must comply with one of the following standards: (1) Comptroller General of the United States; (2) International Organization of Supreme Audit Institutions (INTOSAI); (3) International Auditing Practices Committee of the International Federation of Accountants (IFAC).

Question. The issue of branding—making sure recipients know who is sending the assistance—has been discussed several times before this committee, most recently regarding aid to Syrians.

◆ What is your assessment of the branding of American aid to Syria? Also, please explain our branding efforts globally, including where there are areas for improvement.

Answer. The U.S. Government requires NGO partners to brand our assistance unless doing so would imperil the lives of aid recipients and the humanitarian workers delivering assistance. Recognition of U.S. humanitarian efforts inside Syria is severely constrained by safety and security concerns, but we continue to work to make our humanitarian aid more visible, including some small-scale branding of our assistance. In areas where it is safe to do so, including opposition-held areas in the north; we are able to inform local leaders and recipients about where the aid is coming from. For example, nearly all of the bakeries receiving U.S. Government flour in Aleppo governorate are informed that it is U.S.-donated flour.

Because wide-scale branding is not an option at this time, we are seeking to get the word out in ways that do not undermine the operation: U.S. Government staff in D.C. regularly meet with the Syrian diaspora community to utilize its connections inside Syria and spread the message of USG support. We also continue to heavily engage with local, regional and international media, both traditional and digital, to illustrate the extent to which USG humanitarian assistance is reaching a wide range of areas inside Syria.

In addition, we work with our international organization partners to highlight U.S. Government support wherever possible, and U.S. Government officials use every public opportunity to highlight our humanitarian assistance to the region, including speaking engagements, social media, and regional, national, and international media interviews.

More broadly, since 2004, USAID has significantly improved its branding and marking efforts in order to drive greater awareness of America's support in countries that receive aid ''From the American People.''

Over the past 8 years, we have seen concrete results from our efforts to brand and market USAID's assistance. USAID now has the strongest and most robust branding and marking efforts of all bilateral donors, and we have integrated our branding efforts across our project design and award process to ensure consistency and effectiveness.

USAID's marking requirements, as outlined in the Code of Federal Regulations (22CFR226) and ADS 320 policy guidance, ensure that USAID's visual identity is represented or ''marked'' on all appropriate products: food aid, clinic signs, schools, hospitals, training materials, and other program materials. These federal marking regulations are complemented by our work to ''brand'' USAID assistance—a phrase that broadly encompasses all of our efforts to advance America's strategic priorities abroad by communicating our mission and the investments of the American people around the world.

To put our branding and marking regulations into practice, USAID's overseas communications officers create strategies to tailor messages and information according to each country's specific needs and opportunities. Branding and marking plans, which are required of every USAID contract and grant agreement, further these strategies by outlining how each project will specifically apply federal marking requirements and communicate the message that the assistance is from the American people.

Our communications officers also occasionally direct in-country polling surveys both before and after the communications efforts. Polling data results by region from these surveys offer an important evidence-based review of the impact that can be generated with the consistent application of the USAID brand. The results show that USAID's branding and marking have garnered returns for the United States in terms of awareness and support of our efforts and policies.

Challenges and Solutions to Improving Branding Impact

Despite the progress made by the Agency, challenges remain in our branding and marking efforts and USAID continues to undertake a proactive stance in ensuring branding guidelines are followed. In some parts of the world, the security situation makes marking inherently dangerous to our employees, grantees, and program beneficiaries. In these cases, waivers are sought and granted when situations merit this action.

When USAID observes implementing partners not adhering to branding and marking requirements, we notify these partners in writing of their noncompliance and reiterate the mandatory requirement to observe and apply branding standards. USAID also retains the right to terminate agreements for noncompliance.

Finally, regular polling and surveys of local populations are important tools to understanding the impact and management of our assistance programs in country. Missions also may monitor the local media, and coordinate closely with their respective Embassy Public Affairs Sections, to assess the general sentiment toward USAID's ability to improve host country perception of U.S. political, diplomatic, economic, and security goals in country.

USAID recognizes that effective branding and marking of American assistance abroad can help our Nation achieve its diplomatic, political, economic, and security goals. USAID also works proactively to strengthen efforts to communicate directly to governments, our beneficiaries, and their communities that aid is from the American people.

RESPONSES OF ADMINISTRATOR RAJIV SHAH TO QUESTIONS SUBMITTED BY SENATOR CHRISTOPHER A. COONS

KENYA

Question. I am convinced that USAID's long-term commitment in support of democratic and electoral reform in Kenya made a significant contribution to the largely credible and peaceful election, but the reform process is far from complete and accountability must be strongly enforced.

◆ How will USAID programs help ensure that Kenya continues to implement critical reforms such as devolution, accountability, and land reform?

Answer. Support to the implementation of hard-won reforms will be central to assistance programs in post-election Kenya. USAID programs will continue to assist Kenyans by providing responsive programs which build upon years of partnership. Devolution and accountability will cross-cut all programs, and support for land reform will continue as an integral part of the mission's agriculture programming.

Devolution

Kenya's decision to devolve government systems to the county level will bring governance and service delivery closer to the people served. It will also make decisionmakers more accessible to their constituents. Devolution represents a new operational environment. All of USAID's programming is being adjusted to work with traditional national ministries, new county systems and governance structures, and civil society. The Kenyans are making the adjustments needed across 47 new counties. Most health and education programs were already being implemented by devolved institutions, and the mission is reviewing how it can facilitate the adjustment to county decisionmakers by engaging with the new county governments. This is also true of agriculture programs under Feed the Future. In a targeted governance effort, USAID's democracy, human rights, and governance programs support Kenyans with devolution by assisting national entities facilitating this reform process and providing comprehensive capacity-building for appointed and elected officials. Initial capacity-building has focused on all 47 counties and included training for Governors, Senators, and local assembly representatives. Over the long term, USAID will concentrate resources in 15 to 20 of the newly formed counties—focusing especially on strengthening new women leaders, enhancing public financial management, and combating corruption. Assistance will also target 100 different county-level civil society organizations to strengthen their capacity to oversee local service delivery, ensure accountability, collaborate together, and effectively represent citizen interests (especially those of marginalized groups) in county-level decisionmaking.

Accountability

Because of the high level of corruption in Kenya, USAID strives to build into all of its programs support for transparency and accountability. This is something that relies heavily on both how one does business and what is done. Thus, USAID adheres to regular high standards in program management and oversight through monitoring, evaluating, and auditing. The USAID-funded program, "Strengthening Institutions of Governance and Service Delivery to Entrench Transparency and Accountability," advances the implementation of anticorruption reforms enumerated in Kenya's new constitution, including laws and policies that will reduce corruption throughout the political, electoral, and governance systems in the country. The program increases participation of the various stakeholders in the anticorruption agenda in Kenya by promoting networking among like-minded organizations and state institutions, policy advocacy, and research and documentation. The program also supports research, including institutional systems and practices audits, and systematic monitoring of the performance of key institutions. Central to the program's research work is the annual East African Bribery Index, which documents citizens' experiences with corruption. Research findings are widely disseminated, through stakeholder organizations, the mass media, and social media. The formation of a more effective policy and legal framework has promoted accountability and transparency, resulting in a number of corruption cases that have been investigated, and public resources recovered. For example, recent engagement by Transparency International with the courts helped to clarify that Members of Parliament are constitutionally required to pay taxes and cannot exempt themselves from this responsibility.

USAID's future devolution program also contains several major components that focus on accountability, transparency, and anticorruption. Technical assistance will be provided to county governments to help them set up transparency mechanisms such as the adoption of freedom of information policies and ensuring that government proceedings are shared with the public. The program will also support the adoption of strong procurement, public financial management, and public engagement mechanisms. On the demand side, the program supports civil society and the media to advocate for reform, as well as to monitor county governments through instruments such as citizen scorecards and investigative journalism.

Land Reform

USAID engaged in land reform after the 2007 post-election violence, when no other donor viewed it as feasible. USAID established a pilot community land rights recognition model on the island of Lamu that the Ministry of Lands (MoL) adopted as part of its drafting of the new land laws. After the passage of the 2010 constitution, USAID supported the MoL and the Attorney General's office to draft three new pieces of land legislation that passed in 2012. After executive branch delays, members of the new, constitutionally mandated National Land Commission, which was established by one of the pieces of legislation, were named. In addition, USAID supported women's land rights in the contentious Mau Forest region, helping to empower women in that community and securing better livelihood options for them and their families. USAID continues to support the establishment of the National Land Commission, as well as drafting of the important Community Land Rights Recognition Act, because it will bring transparency to the regulations that govern over 60 percent of Kenya's lands. USAID will also continue to support community-based wildlife conservation, since 60 percent of Kenya's wildlife resides on these communal lands.

USAID's Kenya Civil Society Strengthening Program works with hundreds of civil society organizations to help them effectively advocate for governance reforms, conduct civic education and peace-building activities, and improve management of natural resources. The program provided subgrants, totaling over $27 million, to 260 organizations working to advocate for and monitor progress on important issues, including: elections; ethics and anticorruption; land; human rights; devolution; the police; judiciary; rights for women, youth and persons with disabilities; peace-building; and natural resource management. The program also assisted civil society to provide input and advocacy on key pieces of reform legislation. Legislation successfully enacted include: Truth, Justice and Reconciliation Bill; National Land Policy; Political Parties Bill; Elections Bill; Forest Act; and Wildlife Policy Bill. Partners continue to monitor implementation of these new laws. More than 5,000 people benefited from the improved management of more than half a million hectares of land. The program has created viable, profitable nature-based enterprises and natural resource management activities.

In addition, USAID's Land and Conflict Sensitive Journalism activity has trained dozens of news media representatives on more conflict-sensitive and objective reporting. Land reform, as a major source of livelihoods and of conflict in Kenya, has been a recurring theme covered by the activity.

DEMOCRATIC REPUBLIC OF CONGO (DRC)

Question. Recent developments in the DRC—such as the signing of a multilateral Framework Agreement, appointment of a U.N. envoy, and the expanded mandate of MONUSCO with an intervention force—present an opportunity to make meaningful progress toward sustainable peace.

◆ What is USAID's role and to what extent is the DRC able to effectively absorb more U.S. assistance in light of its significant governance challenges?

Answer. As it becomes clearer how the Peace, Security and Cooperation (PSC) Framework Agreement and authorization of the Intervention Brigade will influence the situation in eastern DRC, USAID will be ready to assist the Congolese people through humanitarian assistance, recovery and development programs specific to eastern DRC, and programs with a broader national coverage that includes, but are not limited to, the east. In FY 2012, USAID programmed approximately $168 million dollars in the region. USAID can also provide strategic analysis of drivers of conflict. Such analysis would help inform the design of strategies and activities to address the root causes of conflict.

It is our judgment that the DRC is able to absorb all of the assistance that the United States has requested. USAID will increasingly implement its programs in alignment with DRC Government priorities and in concert with Congolese partners. This will be a means to build local and national government capacity, strengthen civil society, and foster communication with and accountability to citizens, thus promoting the sustainability of service delivery and building state legitimacy.

We will continue to press the DRC to undertake much-needed domestic reforms, including comprehensive security sector reform, as it committed to do in the PSC Framework. USAID will increase efforts to help the Government of the DRC (GDRC) implement decentralization, as envisioned in the 2006 constitution. Much remains to be done, including putting in place enabling legislation, establishing new institutions, and training officials. USAID and State will coordinate with stakeholders to promote electoral reform and support the GDRC to undertake credible, transparent, and peaceful elections—provincial and local as soon as feasible, and national in 2016.

In eastern DRC, USAID already works with communities to reconcile underlying causes of political and socioeconomic disputes; helps extend state authority through work with local governments; and increases communities' capacity to respond to insecurity. USAID also focuses on sexual and gender-based violence preventative programs and reinforcing communities' capacity to combat sexual violence themselves. In addition, USAID projects provide psychosocial and economic support to allow victims to reenter society.

USAID is helping to develop a mineral traceability program that monitors minerals from the mine to the manufacturing user, ensuring that the minerals do not help fund conflict. USAID and the Department of State will build on recent successes and continue working with private sector partners to demonstrate that legal, responsible, and economically viable trade in natural resources is not only possible but can be beneficial to all stakeholders in a given supply chain. As security in the east increases, these efforts can be expanded to benefit more communities and miners. This expansion will give the diverse actors who currently exploit the absence of state authority a vested interest in supporting improvements to the DRC's stability.

RESPONSES OF ADMINISTRATOR RAJIV SHAH TO QUESTIONS SUBMITTED BY SENATOR JEFF FLAKE

Question. A school of thought exists which posits that U.S. foreign assistance is only effective for countries that want to change.

◆ To what degree do the programs administered by USAID take this into consideration?
◆ The Millennium Challenge Corporation (MCC) has a pretty good success record, and is an organization that firmly subscribes to this school of thought. Can you tell me whether USAID collaborates with MCC on the lessons it has learned in administering foreign assistance?

Answer. USAID subscribes to the view that foreign assistance is most effective when it is given in the context of a full collaboration between the United States and a strong democratic government that is effective on behalf of all its citizens. However, it would not be in the U.S. national interest or comport with American morality to only provide assistance to people fortunate enough to live in countries with such governments. We cannot afford to restrict our fight against global public health threats like HIV/AIDS and multi-drug-resistant tuberculosis to countries that have the best governments, or ignore the plight of sick and starving children because they are not well governed.

USAID has developed effective ways of providing assistance through civil society, NGOs and implementing partners when governments are not the most effective at, or interested in, promoting the welfare of all their citizens, and of promoting improvements in democratic rights and governance that over time will produce better development prospects as well as a more secure world. MCC fills an important niche in U.S. Foreign Assistance. There is a healthy interchange between MCC and USAID on issues of aid effectiveness, and USAID and MCC perform complementary roles in the countries where both operate.

USE OF OCO FUNDS

Question. FY 2012 was the first year that OCO funds were requested for State & Foreign Operations. In that year, Congress provided an additional $2.5 billion in OCO funds above what the administration requested for things like USAID operating expenses, and international development assistance.

- ♦ Given that OCO funds are extra-budgetary and do not count toward overall spending caps set forth by the BCA, does the addition of funds help or hinder USAID's future years budgeting process?
- ♦ Is it common that USAID would try and expend all these dollars to demonstrate a need for them in the next budget year?
- ♦ How does USAID define ''Overseas Contingency Operations?''
- ♦ Does USAID plan to cease the request of OCO funds, commensurate with the timetable for withdrawal from Afghanistan?

Answer. The FY 2014 OCO request funds the extraordinary, but temporary, costs of the Department of State and the U.S. Agency for International Development (USAID) operations in the Frontline States of Iraq, Afghanistan, and Pakistan. This approach to funding extraordinary but temporary costs, which is similar to the approach taken by the Department of Defense, allows USAID and the Department of State to clearly identify the exceptional costs of operating in these countries that are focal points of U.S national security policy and require a significant U.S. civilian presence.

The administration continues to propose a multiyear cap that limits government-wide OCO funding to $450 billion over the 2013 to 2021 period. FY 2014 OCO funding will provide resources for the United States continuing diplomatic platform and foreign assistance programs, including assistance focused on foundational investments in economic growth, support of the military, political and economic transitions, and continuing the capacity-building within the Afghan Government to sustain remarkable gains made in the past decade.

It is certainly not USAID's practice to seek to expend all OCO funding to demonstrate a need for such funding in the next budget year. USAID's assistance programs in Afghanistan, particularly those funded by OCO, are designed through close civilian-military cooperation to ensure collaboration and coordination and a cohesive effort in support of overarching stabilization and development objectives in Afghanistan. They are also designed and implemented in accordance with the Administrator's Sustainability Guidance for USAID in Afghanistan: http://transition.usaid.gov/locations/afghanistanpakistan/documents/afghanistan/sustainabilitylguidancel final.pdf.

CONTRACTING AT USAID

Question. An October 2012 memorandum from the Office of the Inspector General at USAID to your office noted some ongoing issues with projects USAID has been managing. For example, in Afghanistan, ''forty percent of the reports issued from October 1, 2010, through June 30, 2012, have identified contract or project management deficiencies and noncompliance with relevant procedures or regulations.'' In Pakistan, ''more than 40 percent have found internal control weaknesses and noncompliance with relevant procedures or regulations.'' In light of these persistent performance management issues:

- ♦ If a project does not meet specific criteria within its first year, what is USAID's plan for course correction?
- ♦ What are the baselines that Congress should use when evaluating whether USAID is meeting the goals set out for particular projects?
- ♦ How heavily is performance history weighed when USAID is considering awarding a contract to a particular entity?

Answer. USAID staff develop detailed monitoring and evaluation plans as part of their project design process. The targets set in the project monitoring and evaluation plans are the basis for portfolio reviews of progress or lack thereof against targets, during which mission staff make appropriate course correction according to the context.

USAID continues to make strides in its ability to effectively monitor and evaluate its development assistance programs. The Agency has many mechanisms through which it sets targets and collects performance information against those targets. The Agency has revised its guidance on performance monitoring, requiring that missions develop a Project Monitoring and Evaluation (M&E) Plan during the design of new projects. This Project M&E Plan provides a framework for collecting baseline data as well as monitoring project performance during implementation. It is the baselines established for various project level indicators that missions then use during periodic reviews of project implementation to determine whether projects are meeting the targets that have been set against their baselines.

USAID recently updated guidance on past performance tracking as a mandatory reference document to the Automated Directives System (ADS) Chapter 302 with a suggested weight of 20–30 percent.